RAILWAY POSTERS 1923–1947

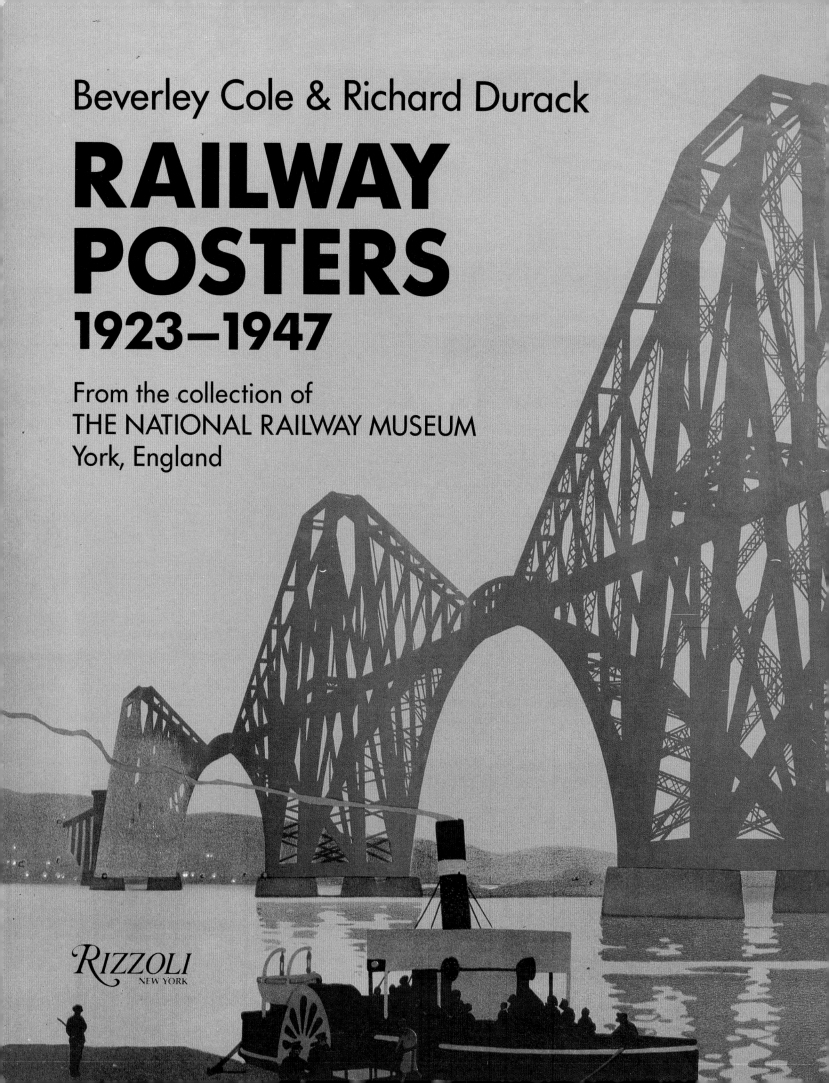

Beverley Cole & Richard Durack

RAILWAY POSTERS
1923–1947

From the collection of
THE NATIONAL RAILWAY MUSEUM
York, England

RIZZOLI
NEW YORK

First published in the United States of
America in 1992 by
Rizzoli International Publications Inc.,
300 Park Avenue South,
New York, NY 10010

Illustrations and text © 1992 National
Railway Museum, York

**Library of Congress
Cataloging-in-Publication Data**
Cole, Beverley.
  Railway posters, 1923–1947 :
  from the collection of the National Railway
  Museum, York, England / Beverley Cole
  and Richard Durack.
    p.   cm.
  ISBN 0–8478–1506–4 (paper)
  1. Railroads–Great Britain–Posters–
  Catalogs.   2. Posters,
  British–Catalogs.   3. Posters–
  20th century–Great Britain–Catalogs.
  4. Posters–England–York–Catalogs.
  5. National Railway Museum–Catalogs.
  I. Durack, Richard.   II. Title.
  NC1849.R34C65 1992
  741.6′74′0941–dc20   91–50830 CIP

This book was designed and produced by
Calmann & King Ltd, London

Designed by Richard Foenander
Printed in Singapore by Toppan Ltd

COVER: Progress Posters No.2 "Steam!" by
T.D. Kerr (1925)
HALF-TITLE: "'The Coronation' Crossing the
Royal Border Bridge" by Tom Purvis (1937)
BACK COVER: "Southern Ireland" by Warwick
Goble (c.1931)

Acknowledgements
Thanks to all our colleagues at the National Railway
Museum who have helped us produce this book,
especially to Lynn Patrick, for photographing the
posters with patience and diplomacy, and to Christine
Heap and Dr John Coiley for reading the manuscript
and offering general encouragement and support.

The National Railway Museum, York, England, opened
to the public in 1975 with collections inherited from its
two constituent organizations, the Railway Museum,
York and the Museum of British Transport in London.

The posters in this book are part of the Museum's
outstanding collection of railway posters which now
numbers over 6,000 and includes examples dating from
the late nineteenth century to the present day. The
posters are all either quad royal size (40 × 50in/101.6 ×
127cm) or double royal size (40 × 25in/101.6 × 63.5cm).
The dates given for each poster are those when it is
known to have been on display. This was usually the
date when the poster was first issued, although posters
were often reprinted, and the same design could
remain on display for many years or reappear after an
absence of some years. Where the date of display is not
known, an approximate date is given.

CONTENTS

INTRODUCTION 6

THE GREAT WESTERN RAILWAY 28

THE SOUTHERN RAILWAY 60

THE LONDON MIDLAND & SCOTTISH RAILWAY 92

THE LONDON & NORTH EASTERN RAILWAY 124

NOTES ON ARTISTS 154

FURTHER READING 158

MUSEUM REFERENCE NUMBERS 159

INTRODUCTION

"This is the day of the poster" wrote Sydney R. Jones in his book *Posters and their Designers* (1924), and nowhere was this more true than in the case of the British railway poster which really came of age in the years before the Second World War. Each of the four railway companies that were formed in 1923 – the Great Western Railway (GWR), Southern Railway (SR), London Midland and Scottish Railway (LMS) and London and North Eastern Railway (LNER) – developed its own style in poster work. Some of the finest poster artists of the day were employed to tempt passengers on to trains. Bathing belles and sunny beaches became a familiar sight on station platforms and jostled for space with more sober images of mines and steelworks. Colourful landscapes designed to appeal to the rambler, healthy spas for invalids and the picturesque ruins of abbeys and castles all tried to entice passengers away from the grime of towns and cities. Views of ships and hotels, and more mundane images of goods depots and furniture vans, provided a reminder that railways went beyond the simple business of running trains, while streamlined expresses and smart new electric trains pointed the way to an exciting future.

In an address to the Hull Advertising Club in 1928, Francis Goodricke, who worked in the LNER advertising department, enthused about the poster: "If for a moment it could be supposed that pictorial posters had no advertising value, their decorative value alone would justify their production" (*Railway Gazette* 7 December). The railway companies never intended their posters to be merely decorative, but they were not slow to realize that a successful poster relied on good design and a strong image for its appeal. The examples in this book, taken from the collection at the National Railway Museum in York, show how effective they were.

THE NEW COMPANIES

The creation of the four new companies on 1 January 1923 followed uncertainty about what to do with the system in the years after the First World War. The railway network itself had grown rapidly during the nineteenth century but in a disorganized way. Lines were built and operated by private companies and there was much overlapping of territory and duplication of routes. Areas were often served by more than one company – while competition was beneficial in many cases, it was wasteful in others and weakened the companies concerned where there was insufficient demand for services. The companies did co-operate in many ways, but by the early years of the twentieth century there were still well over a hundred of varying size providing services. During the First World War the Government took control of the network, although it left the running of it to a Railway Executive Committee composed of professional railwaymen. The war left the railways badly run down, but the benefits of closer working and a unified network had become apparent. Calls for nationalization were resisted and Parliament passed the Railways Act instead in 1921. This forced the companies into four new groups based largely on geographical areas.

In size and character the four companies were very different. The Great Western, which was the only one to retain its former name, was amalgamated with the Cambrian Railways and the companies of the Welsh valleys. It covered the west of England and also provided services in the West Midlands and Wales. The Southern, the smallest of the four, served the area to the south of London but extended as far west as Devon and Cornwall. It had a heavy network of commuter lines and also relied on its continental traffic. The two remaining companies were larger. The London Midland and Scottish Railway, the largest of all, covered mainly the western side of England and included among its constituent companies the London and North Western Railway, Lancashire and Yorkshire Railway and Midland Railway. It extended into Wales as far as Holyhead and into Scotland as far as Thurso where it covered the areas formerly served by the Caledonian Railway, Highland Railway and Glasgow and South Western Railway. The London and North Eastern Railway served largely the eastern side of England. It also provided services in Scotland as far north as the Moray Firth where it took over the systems of the North British Railway and Great North of Scotland Railway. In addition to the four new companies, a number of lines were taken into joint ownership, while several smaller concerns remained unaffected by the amalgamation.

The new arrangements brought a greater degree of unity to the network and made life easier for the traveller. But it had not been the intention of the Act to eliminate competition entirely. The old companies had been amalgamated rather than dismembered, so there was still an overlapping of areas and duplication of lines, albeit on a lesser scale. Both the Great Western and the LMS, for example, continued to compete for traffic on their routes between London and Birmingham in the way that their predecessors, the former Great Western and London and North Western, had

"Hornsea" by C.W. Loten (1911). This technique of showing a series of small views of a resort or region is typical of early railway posters.

companies there was disagreement over several matters, including display space and interior arrangements. The Royal Institute of British Architects was approached and a competition devised with ten judges, two from the Institute and two from each of the companies. The winning design became standard for all offices and the first opened at Queensway, London in 1938.

THE RISE OF THE RAILWAY POSTER

The railway poster was not new in 1923. It had made its first appearance in the later years of the nineteenth century, although the companies had publicized their services from the very early days. They had used the letterpress notice which had become an increasingly elaborate affair, especially where it advertised excursions and special trains. It had its limitations, however, and when developments in colour lithography enabled the pictorial poster to become a cheap and effective form of advertising the companies adopted it – with varying degrees of enthusiasm. Their first efforts were uninspiring: the general idea was to crowd as much information on to the poster as possible. Most posters were used to promote resorts and often consisted of a series of views with lettering that was badly arranged and difficult to read.

Gradually a more professional approach began to emerge. Several companies created their own advertising departments and began to produce co-ordinated campaigns based on a variety of publicity material. Posters improved in both image and content, while lettering was used to much more telling effect to get the message across. The years before the First World War saw the emergence of the "railway advertising man" and there were long debates in the pages of the *Railway Gazette* on whether his value was properly appreciated. Railway advertising enjoyed a higher profile but the standard still varied greatly from company to company. Several, including the Great Central Railway and London and North Western Railway, produced work of a consistently high standard, but the output of many remained predictable and hardly improved over the years. The outbreak of war in 1914 brought advertising to a temporary halt and the companies had barely got back into their stride when the amalgamation took place. Most of the advertising men appointed by the new companies were transferred from the old companies and they were to play a major role in influencing future policy. Some, like William

done. Nevertheless, the general move was towards greater co-operation, especially during the 1930s as the economic slump and increasing challenge from other forms of transport began to bite into the profits of the companies. Through carriages and trains, which travelled from the system of one company to another, had been a feature of the pre-war years and these continued into the new era, with trains such as the *Sunny South Express* carrying holiday-makers from the towns of the north to the south-coast resorts.

At the same time joint advertising became more common. The Great Western joined forces with the LMS to issue a series of posters by Claude Buckle featuring the cathedrals of Gloucester, Hereford and Worcester, and with the Southern to promote Plymouth and South Devon (pages 38–9, 56, 57). The LMS and LNER put their co-operation on a more formal footing in 1931, and there was much joint promotion, especially to destinations in Scotland and resorts served by both companies such as Cromer and Southend. But it was not all plain sailing. When the companies decided that the publicity offices they operated, of which there were over eighty in London alone, should be converted for use by all four

Teasdale at the LNER, soon proved what they could do when given their chance on a wider stage. Others took their old habits with them and their new employers suffered as a result.

Outside influences were important, especially the work of Frank Pick at the Underground Group of companies in London. Pick joined the Underground Group in 1906 and, two years later, was given responsibility for improving its poor public image. One of his first steps had been to introduce a poster advertising campaign with the intention of publicizing services and encouraging travel. Over the years this developed in scope, both in the range of artists employed and the variety of work produced, and it had the side-effect that the Underground gained a reputation as an important art patron.

Pick, however, did not see the poster as an end in itself. He was particularly concerned about the way in which information was presented to passengers and saw little point in producing good posters if they could not be easily seen and read. Display areas were set apart at stations so that Underground publicity did not get lost amongst the general mass of advertising material. The Underground also developed its own typeface which was used on posters, notices and station signs. Pick made no secret of the fact that he was not only encouraging travel but also trying to create goodwill and a better understanding between the passenger and the Underground. By providing clear information on services, and on how they were being improved, he wanted to make the passenger feel an important part of the system. He used a variety of publicity material to achieve his aims, including regular press advertising.

The achievements of the Underground encouraged a new approach to publicity which began to grow in importance during the 1920s. What was described by Walter Shaw Sparrow in 1924 as the "reform movement in advertising" gained greater acceptance. A new breed of poster artist began to emerge who emphasized the need for good design and imaginative use of colour and saw the cluttered images on most posters as a thing of the past. This new approach had a varying impact on the railway companies. It had its greatest effect on the Southern and the LNER. It had less influence on the LMS which chose to follow its own very different course. The Great Western allowed itself to be hardly affected at all and was a notable absentee from the increasing amount of literature on advertising and poster art that was published during this period.

One of the Great Western's first posters showed Eileen Nolan and her sister Peggy braving the sea at St Agnes in 1923.

GO GREAT WESTERN

The Great Western had never been noted for the quality of its posters and the first efforts of the new company were hardly inspiring. In February 1923 it issued "Bathing in February in the Cornish Riviera" which featured a set of five black-and-white photographs of Miss Eileen Nolan and her sister Peggy bathing in the sea at St Agnes. The Great Western had always promoted the mild climate of Cornwall as suitable for winter holidays, but did not usually go as far as encouraging its passengers to swim. The photographs had originally appeared in the *Daily Mirror*, and the *Railway Gazette* was at pains to emphasize that this was not just a publicity stunt. It pointed out to its readers that Miss Nolan and her sister had been

"bathing regularly for some time" when the photographs were taken (*Railway Gazette* 9 March). The Great Western largely confined its poster advertising to resorts and holiday areas, with few new ideas. Some progress was made with designs by Fred Taylor, and the landscapes of F. J. Widgery and L. Burleigh Bruhl (pages 30–31) had their devotees, but in general Great Western posters had an old-fashioned feel that compared unfavourably with the work being produced by the other companies. With their poor images and clumsy lettering they lacked both imagination and style.

This approach contrasted sharply with the general attitude of the Great Western to publicity, a subject it had always taken seriously. Much of the other material it issued was of a high standard, notably its impressive range of handbooks and guides. This policy was upheld by the new company. In the same year that the Nolan sisters were bathing in Cornwall, it issued *The 10.30 Ltd*, described as "A Railway Book for Boys of All Ages". The book was written by W. G. Chapman and described the journey from London to Plymouth in terms of railway operation and equipment rather than the scenic delights that could be seen along the line. Publication was followed by an essay competition on the subject "What I know about Railways" which was open to girls as well as boys. Almost a quarter of the essays did in fact come from girls and this caused some surprise!

In 1924 the Great Western expanded its Advertising Department and renamed it the Publicity Department. William Fraser, an employee for over thirty years, was appointed Publicity Agent and the publications programme was expanded still further. Chapman went on to write several further volumes on railway subjects and the company also moved into new areas of publicity including the sale of jigsaw puzzles. This increased level of activity had little effect on poster advertising, however, which in terms of quality remained a neglected field.

The reasons for this are not difficult to understand. Unlike the other companies the Great Western did not suffer a major upheaval in 1923. It continued much as before and this applied as much to publicity as to its other areas of activity. Its strengths carried over, but so too did its weaknesses. In the case of posters the weaknesses included over-reliance on printing firms and the frequent concern for economy above all else which led to designs of poor quality.

Moreover, the Great Western had never been convinced of the value of the poster over other forms of advertising and this attitude persisted. D. Richards, speaking in 1925 to the Great Western Railway Lecture and Debating Society, condemned what he called the "too common use of the poster" and went on: "Admittedly, the railway poster possesses a value both of site and of public attention that is peculiar to itself, but I am sure you cannot expect to tell the public all you

want to, or even to induce any part of the public to travel, by means of the poster alone....The poster, in any field of advertising, must always be complimentary to the press, and in my view railway companies have been much too prone to put all, or nearly all, their eggs in one basket. It is a fact, however, that the past few months have, in the instance of at least one great railway, seen a departure, and I believe that if the railways would tell their public in the press some of the things they endeavour to tell them by poster, they would achieve a much larger measure of real and useful publicity" (*Railway Gazette* 13 February). The Great Western had always placed a great reliance on the press. It regularly advertised its services and excursion trains in both national and provincial newspapers and backed up its announcements with notices and handbills. This policy continued with the new company and while it lasted the poster was to remain a low priority.

Attitudes began to change in the 1930s as the Great Western made a belated attempt to catch up with its rivals. Fraser retired in 1931 and was replaced by Keith Grand, his assistant, who introduced a number of improvements in poster design. The roundel monogram began to appear regularly on posters and other publicity material to identify it immediately as Great Western, and lettering was made clearer to detract less from the image. Grand was promoted two years later and replaced by M. J. Dewar who was appointed from outside the company and had a background in publicity. Dewar continued the improvements in poster advertising and pursued a more adventurous policy. The output of posters increased as they began to play a greater role in Great Western publicity efforts and some very fine designs were produced during the remaining years of the company.

In 1933 a series of six posters of Devon and Cornwall was commissioned from the American designer Edward McKnight Kauffer (page 40). He was highly regarded by the new school of poster artists and by the critics but his designs were not to everyone's taste. His posters of Devon and Cornwall caused much comment, not all of it favourable, but this did not stop the Great Western commissioning a further design of Windsor from him two years later (page 43). Further innovation followed in 1936 with the appearance of a series of posters by Ronald Lampitt in an unusual mosaic style (page 44). The subjects again included Devon and Cornwall and they were much admired.

In addition to new designs and novel ideas the Great Western drew on its own resources. This had not always had happy results in the past, and had led to amateurish publicity, but in Charles Mayo they found an artist who was responsible for several successful designs. Mayo had joined the Publicity Department in 1932 and was responsible for producing artwork for posters and book covers. In 1939 he produced the most famous Great

Western poster of all in "Speed to the West" (page 52), a striking view from ground level of a "King" class locomotive on a west of England holiday express. Mayo also designed a number of other posters including views of Windsor and Cheddar Gorge. The latter formed part of the "This England of Ours" series which marked a new approach by the company to architectural and landscape subjects. Many fine landscape posters were produced during the 1930s, including work by Alker Tripp, Leonard Richmond and Claude Buckle. During its final years the Great Western also commissioned designs from Frank Mason and Frank Newbould, both of whom had established their reputations with their work for the LNER.

THE WAY OF PROGRESS

Life was not so easy for the Southern Railway. Relations between its three constituent companies had never been good and it took some time to establish a degree of unity. This led to a delay in filling appointments and it was not until October 1923 that, in the true spirit of compromise, Fred Milton of the London and South Western Railway was made Chief of the Publicity Section, while George Dennis of the London Brighton and South Coast Railway was appointed Chief of the Advertising Section. Before this the Southern had continued much as before with three sections, instead of the three constituent companies, issuing publicity material. The South Western Section, which served the area of the former London and South Western Railway, was the most active and produced several posters, including a colourful view of the coastal scenery of Dorset (page 62). The distinction between the sections was soon dropped, and in 1924 the Southern began to issue a series of landscape posters by Donald Maxwell which were intended to cover the whole of the system. The first appeared with the title "The Lake District of Surrey" (page 62) and further views of Kent, Cornwall, London, Sussex and Somerset followed over the next two years. Maxwell was to become a regular artist for the Southern, producing carriage prints and illustrations for guidebooks, as well as posters.

But just as Southern advertising was getting into its stride there was a sudden change of policy. This was brought about by criticism of its suburban services which increased in intensity during 1924. The companies that formed the Southern had been no strangers to criticism; the South Eastern and Chatham Railway in particular had been a constant source of unhappiness to its passengers. The complaints ranged from increased overcrowding and the poor quality of carriages to dissatisfaction caused by a rationalization of services. The company had begun a programme of improve-

ments, including further electrification, but its response was low-key. It did little to publicize the changes, with the result that complaints mounted as the improvement work itself caused further delays. The problem was essentially one of communication, so the Southern decided to remedy it by embarking on what the *Railway Gazette* was later to describe as a "systematic scheme of connected and co-related publicity" that would open the way for "the carrying out of a definite scheme of propaganda designed to develop kinship of interests between public and railway" (7 January 1927).

This was very much the Underground approach and had in fact been recommended to the Southern by Lord Ashfield, Chairman of the Underground Group of companies. Ashfield also suggested the appointment of John Elliot, who had worked for the *New York Times* and *London Evening Standard*, to develop and control the campaign; he joined the Southern in January 1925 as Public Relations Assistant to the General Manager. He pursued his aims in two ways: he launched an advertising campaign in newspapers and magazines, and set about improving relations with the press.

The first advertisement in the newspaper campaign appeared under the heading "The Truth about the Southern" and reviewed the role and achievements of its constituent companies during the First World War. It went on to outline the improvements that were being introduced and was accompanied by the slogan "Southern Railway – Actively Engaged in the Public Service" which came to be used regularly. "The Truth about the Southern" was followed up with a further series of press announcements under the general title "Telling the Public". These provided information on a range of subjects. Details of suburban electrification and the building of new steam locomotives shared space with accounts of how carriages were cleaned and the difficulties of dealing with rush-hour traffic. As the campaign extended further, new slogans began to appear. Announcements on electrification, which were always given a high profile, were issued under headings which included "The Way of Progress" and "A Greater Electric", while general information on services often used the title "Facts for Fair-Minded People".

Elliot saw the improvement of relations with the press as equally important. He opened an Information Section at Waterloo which reporters were free to visit and provided regular articles and information. He paid particular attention to suburban and evening newspapers as these had been responsible for much of the criticism of the Southern. The new approach to press relations was extremely successful; the better understanding that resulted was to last until the Second World War and beyond.

Other forms of publicity played their part in the campaign. Folders with the title "On the Upgrade" were issued to passengers, and a regular publication called "Over the Points" was produced for first-class season ticket holders. A series of four "Progress" posters was designed by T. D. Kerr (pages 64–5) which again outlined the modernization that was taking place. The Southern also showed great imagination in following up subjects to create further publicity. When the "King Arthur" class locomotives appeared, interest was built up through a series of press announcements which began in February 1925. The locomotives were given names taken from *Le Morte d'Arthur* by Sir Thomas Malory. This also helped to publicize the area of North Cornwall around Tintagel which was served by the Southern. The first appearance of the locomotive *King Arthur* at Waterloo received a great deal of coverage and the Southern went on to produce booklets, postcards and even paperweights which sold in large numbers.

The success of the propaganda campaign set new standards for the Southern's advertising generally. The importance of using a variety of publicity material in a co-ordinated way had become apparent, as had the need for good press and public relations. Poster design was the next area for improvement. Elliot, who had been made responsible for all publicity and advertising in January 1926, again sought inspiration from the Underground and also from the LNER. He introduced a poster advertising programme and commissioned work from many artists new to the Southern including Ethelbert White and Gregory Brown. Electrification continued to receive a great deal of publicity and, as the suburban programme gave way to the schemes on longer routes during the 1930s, each new opening was marked by an advertising campaign in which posters played a major role. In 1933 the line to Brighton was electrified and, in addition to the routine publicity, the Southern took the opportunity the following year of changing the name of its popular *Southern Belle* to the *Brighton Belle* and styling it the "All-Pullman Electric". In 1937 the route to Portsmouth and Southsea followed and for this the Southern issued a fine poster by Charles Pears featuring one of their new electric trains in a wooded setting (page 85).

Many stations were rebuilt and modernized, and as both services and facilities improved, the number of passengers increased. London was easier to reach and it became possible to live well away from the city yet still commute comfortably. Much advertising was aimed at the commuter but the Southern was also keen to promote off-peak travel by shoppers and theatre-goers, as well as encouraging Londoners to visit the country-

side. The image of the Southern was transformed during these years. The slogan "Southern Electric" was used on stations, bridges and posters to advertise the new network. The work of artists, including Edmond Vaughan and V. L. Danvers, emphasized the speed, comfort and frequency of the new services. The Southern established itself as a modern, progressive railway, with reliable and fast electric trains.

This new image did not mean that the more traditional area of holiday publicity was neglected: the Southern developed its own style in advertising resorts both at home and abroad. Much of its output was brash and unsophisticated, but highly effective. The "Southern Coast" was promoted as the sunshine coast and colourful characters were used to reinforce this theme. Both the little boy standing at the end of the platform and Sunny South Sam appeared regularly and achieved great popularity (pages 77, 88). The posters issued for resorts were often dull by comparison. Some good work was done by artists such as Kenneth Shoesmith and V. L. Danvers but there were few beach scenes and designs were largely restricted to general views. The Southern

FAR RIGHT The Southern's Sunny South Sam was so popular that he even had his own song, a novelty foxtrot, written by Will E. Haines and Leo Bliss and published with the permission of the Southern. LEFT Not-So-Sunny South Sam? A Southern guard c. 1938.

paid greater attention to advertising its continental services and was able to promote a range of exotic destinations that could be reached via its own ferry services. Glamorous trains were publicized, including the *Golden Arrow* and *Nord Express*, which was promoted in association with railway companies in Belgium, France, Germany and Poland. Much of the advertising of continental services was carried out with other companies, notably the Chemin de Fer du Nord in France, and this enabled the Southern to share in the exciting work that such artists as Cassandre, Biais and Massiot were producing during these years.

"ART ON THE HOARDINGS"

The London Midland and Scottish was a very different railway from the Southern but it too got off to a difficult start. There were not only tensions between several of the constituent companies but also problems in bringing together such a vast and diverse system. Nevertheless, the LMS announced its arrival with a series of press advertisements. Under the heading "Still Better Service" the new company promised that "punctual train services, clean and healthy carriages, good meals nicely served, civility and attention will be known as the distinguishing characteristics of the London Midland and Scottish Railway" (*Railway Gazette* 19 January 1923). Its first posters showed little change from previous years. "Sweet Rothesay Bay", for example, (page 94) was pure Caledonian Railway in style and only the name of the new company provided a reminder that there had been an amalgamation. In

March 1923 T. C. Jeffrey, Superintendent of Advertising with the Midland Railway, was appointed Superintendent of Advertising and Publicity, and LMS advertising began to adopt distinct Midland characteristics. The slogan "The Best Way", used by the Midland for many years, started to appear on posters, as did other features such as the standard use of a crimson border and the Midland style of colouring and lettering. Jeffrey also kept his department at Derby, the former home of the Midland Railway; it was not until his retirement four years later that it moved to the LMS head offices at Euston.

Like the Southern, however, the LMS suddenly changed its policy towards poster advertising, taking a course that was very much its own. It commissioned three posters from the artist Norman Wilkinson and asked for his views on how its advertising could be improved. Wilkinson proposed that, in order to raise standards, members of the Royal Academy should be asked to design a series of posters for the company. He was prepared for criticism – the arguments that high art and commercial art would not mix and that Academicians could not do posters – but, as he later recorded in his autobiography *A Brush with Life*, he thought that the benefits would far outweigh the dangers: "Even though some of the posters might fall short of the qualities usually looked for in posters, there was one outstanding factor which convinced me that I was right. Here was an attempt to put the poster high up on the artistic ladder and the resulting publicity was bound to do something that no amount of commercial advertising could possibly achieve." The LMS accepted the idea and Wilkinson was asked to organize the scheme on their behalf.

LMS CARLISLE
THE GATEWAY TO SCOTLAND.
BY MAURICE GREIFFENHAGEN. R.A.

Maurice Greiffenhagen
CARLISLE – THE GATEWAY TO
SCOTLAND
1924

The most popular poster in the 1924
Royal Academy series, this appealed
both to the public, who bought copies
in large numbers, and to critics. Percy
Bradshaw praised it in his book *Art in
Advertising*: "It is a fine piece of
decoration, it emphasises the romance
of Carlisle and of the district which it is
designed to advertise, and can hold its
own against the simplest and most
forceful of competitive appeals."

LEFT A winning entry by the LMS at the
Blackpool Trade and Commerce
Procession in 1925.

Wilkinson was no newcomer to the railway poster. In
1905 he had produced two posters for the London and
North Western Railway advertising their steamship
route between Holyhead and Dublin. Both were impressive views, largely of sea with the vessels kept in
proportion rather than being drawn out-of-scale to
impress with their size. Lettering was kept to a minimum and was small and simple in treatment. The
newspapers of the day hailed them as the finest
examples yet of "Art on the Hoardings", and Wilkinson
went on to produce further work for the London and
North Western as well as for the Great Eastern Railway.
He did not share the views of the new school of poster
designers. To him the pictorial element was all-
important and, in an interview with *The Observer*,
reported in the *Railway Gazette* in 1923, he saw
advantages in an alternative approach: "There is an
idea very generally entertained that a poster is a
particular form of art, and must be handled on certain
conventional lines. This to me is a fallacy. A poster – I
am speaking now of pictorial posters – is something

that will attract and arrest the attention of the public. It therefore follows that if the bulk of the posters now displayed are on certain lines, one is likely to achieve greater success with something that is not essentially on these lines. Many members of the Royal Academy have never before done a poster. This to me is an excellent reason for expecting from them something new in treatment and unhampered in outlook" (28 December).

Wilkinson was not alone in his views: others were keen to see the work of Academicians on the hoardings. *The Studio*, in its special spring number of 1923, lamented the poor standard of most poster art and called for the creation of a Ministry of Fine, Commercial and Applied Arts which might "induce Sir William Orpen, Mr Augustus John, Mr Munnings or a dozen others to paint something for the poor man's gallery" (*Railway Gazette* 28 December 1923).

Eighteen artists were approached by Wilkinson and all, with the exception of Frank Brangwyn who was working for the LNER, accepted. Most were enthusiastic; Augustus John was the only one who failed to produce a design. The subjects were chosen and allocated by Wilkinson but the artists were then left to carry out the design in their own way. Each was paid a fee of £100 as well as a royalty on any copies that were sold to the public.

The first posters began to appear on the hoardings during the early months of 1924. They were intended to illustrate the life and work of the LMS as well as the scenic areas it served. No less than five featured castles. Four were contributed by Sir David Murray, Julius Ollson, L. Campbell Taylor and Adrian Stokes, but the most impressive was of Nottingham by Arnesby Brown (page 97). Landscapes of the Scottish Highlands and Aberdeen were produced by Sir D. Y. Cameron and Algernon Talmage, while George Henry provided a study of Aberdeen and Charles Sims his own amusing view of London (page 97).

Three posters depicted industries served by the LMS, including "Cotton" by Cayley Robinson (page 14). This was new ground for the railway poster. Companies had in the past advertised docks and other facilities that they offered to industry but had not shown the industries themselves. Wilkinson saw no reason why posters should only show the delights of the Lake District or Scottish Highlands. "Beauty of another kind is to be seen in the great industries of the north," he commented to *The Observer* (*Railway Gazette* 28 December 1923). Like many others he believed that passengers were interested in the work of the railway in all its forms. Similar arguments applied to posters that portrayed the railway itself and two were included as part of the scheme. "The Night Mail" by Sir William Orpen (page 96) showed the crew on the footplate of their locomotive, while "The Permanent Way" by Stanhope Forbes (page 96) featured a track gang at work on the line.

The final two posters in the scheme proved to be both the most unusual and the most popular. "Speed" by Sir Bertram MacKennal (page 97) featured a photograph of a winged figure modelled in low relief in clay. "Carlisle" by Maurice Greiffenhagen (page 13), with its knight in armour mounted on a white horse, was the most successful poster in the series. Percy Bradshaw, writing in *Art in Advertising*, saw it as the only good design to come out of the scheme: "Maurice Greiffenhagen's lifetime of experience as illustrator, decorator, and painter is obvious in this splendid work, compared to which many of the designs of his fellow Academicians, from the poster point of view, look

Cayley Robinson
BRITISH INDUSTRIES – COTTON
1924

One of three posters in the Royal Academy scheme which depicted industries served by the LMS, "Cotton" showed women at work in a Lancashire cotton mill. The company wanted to demonstrate that they were proud of the heavy industries and committed to the common spirit of national production. The other posters were "Coal" by George Clausen, which featured miners and the winding gear of a colliery, and "Steel" by Richard Jack, which showed the furnaces and chimneys of a steelworks near Motherwell in Scotland.

Printed by Eyre & Spottiswoode Ltd

inexperienced and ineffective. Greiffenhagen has realised that a good picture is not necessarily a good poster; his design is both, whereas the other artists have produced designs which do not suggest any special consideration of poster conventions".

The scheme generated an enormous amount of publicity for the LMS as Wilkinson had predicted and, despite the doubts of Bradshaw and others, opinion was largely favourable. Copies of the posters sold well and a calendar and booklet were produced. The original paintings went on show in both Britain and the USA. But above all the scheme really set the tone for the succeeding years. LMS posters projected a sober and dignified image – a little dull perhaps but here was a sensible working railway. The principles established by Wilkinson continued, as did the range of subjects. Landscapes by artists including S. J. Lamorna Birch and Paul Henry shared space with posters featuring industrial and railway themes. Wilkinson went on to produce well over a hundred designs for the company. His best were of shipping subjects but he carried out work of all types with the exception of resorts. Two of his best-known series were of castles and abbeys and of public schools on the LMS (page 122). In both, a brief description of the subject appeared in the text of each poster and this became a standard feature. It was not only used in the work of Wilkinson but also that of several other artists including Christopher Clark.

Not all the work of the LMS was quite so serious. Septimus Scott and Charles Pears showed that the company could produce a good seaside poster when it wanted to, and there were also several lively designs for special events. It often showed imagination in its choice of artists too. Cassandre, Matania and Spencer Pryse were among the artists it used, and towards the end of the 1930s a fine series of posters was commissioned from Bryan de Grineau, including an impressive study of the *Coronation Scot* (page 117).

FORWARD WITH THE LNER

The LNER suffered few of the early conflicts that troubled the Southern and LMS. Relations between the constituent companies were generally amicable and the new company soon got into its stride. A series of notices and press advertisements under the heading "Our Aim is to Serve You" marked its arrival, but it took its most significant step in February 1923 when it appointed William Teasdale as its Advertising Manager. Teasdale had been Trade Advertising Agent with the North Eastern Railway, a company that had set high standards in its poster work and methods of display, and he had definite views on the role of the advertising man. In an address on "Railway Advertising", reported in Bradshaw's *Art in Advertising*, "he reminded his audience that the first problem which besets the railway advertising man is to decide just *what* he is going to advertise. Is he to be content with making his railway known and telling the world what his railway *does*, or preaching what his railway has in the way of equipment? The railway advertising man's difficulty is to dig out from a vast organisation the best selling points."

Good relationships with colleagues were important, but the advertising man had to have complete charge of all advertising: "The various departments must let the advertising manager know the value to the company of the place, district, or services which are to be advertised, and agree in consultation as to the potential value of such services. The advertising department must advise other departments of the amounts which it will be necessary to spend, and put before them in broad outline the method it is proposed to adopt in advertising such places or services. The amounts to be spent should most certainly be subject to negotiation with the departments for whom the advertisements are being issued, but the form which the advertisements take is a matter which rests entirely with the advertising department, and Mr Teasdale insists that, to make advertising successful, it is absolutely necessary that the expert be left to himself."

Teasdale knew exactly what he wanted at the LNER. One of his first steps was to introduce a poster advertising campaign and the new company soon established a reputation for producing exciting and innovative work. "A man of genius in the world of advertising" was the view of Walter Shaw Sparrow and few disagreed as the LNER set a standard in poster design that none of its rivals could match.

Its first poster, issued in March 1923, featured a view by Fred Taylor of the interior of York Minster (page 126). It was much admired. "One of the finest coloured posters ever issued in connection with railway publicity," commented the *Railway Gazette*; "if it may be regarded as a criterion of the posters to come from the same quarter it may confidently be set down as a happy augury" (16 March 1923). It was, and over the next few months a stream of colourful images appeared on the hoardings as the campaign initiated by Teasdale began to get under way. The designs that he commissioned stretched to all corners of the system. Posters of resorts were most numerous and covered the east coast from Southend as far north as Dunbar. Inland and continental attractions were well represented, and Frank Mason contributed a study of dock facilities at Blyth. There was also an example of what was later to be referred to as "reminder advertising" (*Railway Gazette* 16 May 1930), featuring a woodcut of the *Flying Scotsman* by H. L. Oakley with the title "Travel to Scotland by the East Coast Route". Reminder advertising was used by the LNER to provide a constant reminder to passengers about its major routes. Slogans such as "King's Cross for Scotland" and "Harwich for the Continent" were to appear frequently on posters and other publicity material. Several of the artists used by Teasdale during this first year were to work regularly for the LNER, including H. G. Gawthorne, R. E. Higgins and Frank Newbould, in addition to Frank Mason and Fred Taylor.

Teasdale took great care over the artists he commissioned and the subjects he asked them to do. He had no doubts about the relationship between himself and the artists he used. It was his responsibility as Advertising Manager to decide on the type of poster that would most appeal to the public and then, using his knowledge of the artists he knew, to commission a design from the one most likely to produce what was wanted. He saw no harm in suggesting ideas to artists but rarely found it necessary if he had chosen properly. Equal care was taken in matching artist to subject. There was some specialization, with Frank Mason concentrating on marine subjects and Fred Taylor on architectural themes, but in general Teasdale tried to avoid too many similar designs, and artists were not asked to do more than one poster of a resort or holiday area unless they were several years apart. Variety of appeal was important: beach scenes alternated with views of the promenade and other features in order to attract as wide a number of visitors as possible. Over the years artists commissioned by the LNER ranged from the avant-garde to Royal Academicians, including Brangwyn and Laura Knight. Both Teasdale and his successor Cecil Dandridge favoured the new school of designers but were happy to commission work from almost any source if they thought it would achieve results.

In December 1926 Teasdale took the unusual step of offering contracts to five artists if they would agree not to work for any of the other three railway companies. Austin Cooper, Frank Mason, Frank Newbould, Tom Purvis and Fred Taylor had all been working for the LNER for some time, and Teasdale guaranteed to commission posters to a minimum amount from each artist for the three years to the end of 1929. He made it clear that the contracts would make no difference to the relationship between company and artist and that they might not like some of the subjects they were asked to do. All five accepted, with Taylor guaranteed the highest sum of £1,000. During the first year he was asked to complete twelve designs, including a series on historical subjects. Newbould was promised £500 and was asked for five, including posters of Berlin, Flushing

and the *Balkan Express*. He was also asked to visit Dresden, Nuremberg and Vienna to make preliminary designs. Purvis was guaranteed £450, while Cooper and Mason were each promised £350.

The arrangement worked well. When the time came to renew the contracts Teasdale had been promoted to Assistant Manager and replaced by Cecil Dandridge. Teasdale kept an eye on the negotiations, however. He recommended that the contracts be renewed for a further three years but to include publicity material of all kinds, and that all five artists be paid in pounds, not guineas. (Up until then, Newbould, Purvis and Cooper had been paid in guineas for individual designs.) "Commercial artists should welcome this distinction between their own and the Fine Arts," he wrote in a note to Dandridge in November 1929, "and like ordinary businessmen take their payment in pounds only." This ran into trouble with both Cooper and Newbould but both finally agreed. The guaranteed sums were raised and there was also a general increase of 25 per cent in fees, although this varied with each artist. Taylor became the highest paid and received £100 for each quad royal (50 x 40 in) design. Newbould was paid £84,

Tom Purvis in front of one of his own 16-sheet posters.

Cooper £68 and both Mason and Purvis £65 each. Rates for double royal (40 x 25 in) posters were roughly half, while those in 16-sheet size (80 x 120 in) were generally slightly more. The five became in effect house artists to the LNER. In 1931 they offered to reduce their fees by 5 per cent in line with the reduction in wages that company officials had suffered. This was accepted but at the end of 1932 their contracts were not renewed as the LNER, hit by falling revenue, sought to cut its costs. All five continued to work for the company but on a lesser scale.

The scheme had been a great success. The LNER had not only ensured that the core of their poster work was of a consistently high standard, but also that the artists were not able to work for any of their rivals. Taylor was the most popular of the five, and his architectural studies in particular were always much admired, but it was Purvis who received the most critical acclaim both for his boldness and originality. "He understands the value of elimination," wrote a reviewer in *The Observer* on 17 March 1929, "and of reducing every subject to its simplest forms and bare essentials. His effective flat patterns explain themselves in a flash."

The LNER also moved towards greater standardization in its poster design during these years. Teasdale had always been concerned about legibility and the need to keep lettering simple and easy to read. In 1927 he and the five contract artists agreed on measures to make their posters more uniform, including the regular use of the LNER "totem". This had appeared intermittently since 1924, at first with the full name of the company but later abbreviated to initials, and remained in general use until 1928 when it was briefly replaced by the "lozenge" logo. Both Teasdale and Dandridge wanted to create an "LNER look" which was to apply to all publicity material – handbills, leaflets and advertisements as well as posters. This was a huge task as much material was still produced locally, but in 1929 the company decided to commission its own typeface from the designer Eric Gill. In an address to the Institute of Transport in February 1938 Dandridge commented: "LNE Railway Gill Sans is without ornament or serif and represents in any size or weight about the maximum clarity which can be obtained from the printed word." It was applied progressively throughout the system from printed material to signs and streamlined trains. Gill also designed a new "winking eye" logo for the company which first appeared in 1933. It was short-lived, although it was used on booklets and several posters, including "East Coast" by Dorothea Sharp (page 149). In the following year it was replaced by an amended version, with the initials no longer joined, and this remained in widespread use until 1947.

Greater attention was also paid to display. The LNER, together with the other railway companies, produced most of its posters in either quad royal or double royal size. Posters for public hoardings were produced in 16-sheet size and the LNER also made use of long "streamers" which were never less than 100 x 42 in. Hoardings were coded so that posters could be easily sited for best effect and did not get lost among other advertisements. Displays of the work of particular artists were frequently staged at larger stations.

The LNER also produced sets of posters, usually consisting of a series of six and displayed beneath a streamer or lettered heading. Frank Newbould designed two of the most popular in "East Coast Types" and "East Coast Frolics" (page 146), while the work of Austin Cooper was equally good. He contributed several sets including "Olde World Market-Places", "The Booklover's Britain" and "Passengers of the Past" which featured journeys taken by the Pilgrim Fathers, Robinson Crusoe (and Friday), Samuel Pepys, John Gilpin, Admiral Von Tromp and Doctor Johnson. Frank Mason and Frank Taylor produced several sets, but two of the most fascinating came from Tom Purvis. Both "East Coast Joys" (pages 18–19) and "East Coast Resorts" formed one continuous coastline when joined together and looked particularly impressive on the hoardings.

DESIGN AND REACTION

Purvis was one of the most influential members of the new school of poster designers. He held strong views, not only on the need for good design, but also on the value of commercial art as a discipline in its own right. At a time when commercial art was largely unappreciated he argued that his work demanded exactly the same skills, training and knowledge as that of a Royal Academician. In his view the good commercial artist should also be a good salesman, and he emphasized this point in a lecture to the Bradford Publicity Club in February 1929: "Commercial art is the ability of the artist applied to the purposes of commerce – that is like furniture designing or wallpaper designing it is an applied art, art applied to commercial needs. A good commercial artist must be as much a salesman as an artist – at times more of a salesman than an artist. Sad as it may seem to artists he must *never* let his salesmanship be obliterated by his artistic sensibilities. He *must* have a very clear understanding of salesmanship, the final purpose of his work being to attract his audience with his message in such a way as to leave them interested in if not actually convinced of its entire desirability to themselves. His aim must be sure and his judgement unerring, conveying his own complete conviction of the value of his client's commodity. Advertisement designing demands imagination, invention, craftsmanship and salesmanship."

Purvis's views were echoed by many other artists, including Austin Cooper. In *Making A Poster*, published in 1938, Cooper outlined the stages to be followed to produce an effective poster. He too emphasized the need for what Purvis described in *Poster Progress* as "fitness to its purpose", as well as simplicity and clarity in getting the message across. To both artists the necessity of good overall design was far more important than the style of the poster itself.

Style was much discussed by the critics of the period who favoured the work of designers influenced by the various modern art movements of the early twentieth century, including Cassandre and McKnight Kauffer, at the expense of Purvis and others. Cooper described the

two styles as "abstract and realistic" and discussed the advantages and disadvantages of both. He defined abstract as depending for its effect "upon the suggestion of ideas in decorative form and by way of symbolism" and realistic "upon the presentation of more or less familiar forms in a pictorial way", before putting the view of the practical poster designer: "Both types of poster are useful – both have their devotees. There are occasions when either one of these treatments is more suitable than the other. Both types can fail to function successfully for quite opposite reasons. Only too often we find realistic posters that really belong to the category of easel-pictures or magazine illustrations.... On the other hand we find abstract designs used for propaganda that puzzle us by being recondite and incoherent or fail to attract us by their lack of human warmth. The student must steer somewhere between these extremes. The too familiar leads to banality; the unintelligible is only an arrogance."

Much of this debate passed the passenger by, although few can have failed to notice the changes that were taking place on the hoardings. The companies were keen to encourage this interest and made copies of posters available to the public which sold well. They also kept their employees informed: articles on publicity began to appear in their own staff magazines. In 1923 the LNER took the poster out of the station and

Nº 1 WALKING TOURS

EAST COAST JOYS
travel by L·N·E·R
TO THE DRIER SIDE OF BRITAIN

Nº 2 SUN-BATHING

EAST COAST JOYS
travel by L·N·E·R
TO THE DRIER SIDE OF BRITAIN

Nº 3 SAFE SANDS

EAST COAST JOYS
travel by L·N·E·R
TO THE DRIER SIDE OF BRITAIN

A corner of the LNER Exhibition of Poster Art at the New Burlington Galleries, London c. 1928.

Tom Purvis
EAST COAST JOYS
1931
The six posters in this series form a continuous scene when placed next to each other, but each poster is so designed that it can also stand alone.

into the gallery by mounting the first of a series of poster exhibitions, staged in the Board Room at King's Cross. Forty posters were put on display, together with other designs. It proved to be a great success and became an annual event before moving to the New Burlington Galleries in 1928. This more than doubled the space available and over the next few years the LNER mounted some of its most impressive displays.

In the Eleventh Exhibition of Poster Art in 1933, over sixty posters were put on show, including sets by Frank Mason and Tom Purvis, in addition to "East Coast Frolics" by Frank Newbould (page 146) and the LNER "Chef and Waiter" ("Perfection"/"Discretion") by Austin Cooper (page 143). There were studies of the Cruden Bay Hotel and Great Eastern Hotel by Gordon Nicoll (page 150), as well as two freight studies, including "Capacity-Mobility on the LNER" by H. G. Gawthorn (page 139). Ludwig Hohlwein contributed three posters, including a view of Edinburgh, and the exhibition saw the welcome return of John Hassall's "Jolly Fisherman" from Skegness in a revised design (page 149). There were also twenty-two original designs on display, including work by Dorothea Sharp, Henry Rushbury, Fred Taylor and Alexander Alexieff, in addition to notices, newspaper advertisements, etchings for restaurant car menus and twelve poster designs submitted by students of the Royal College of Art. The exhibition was opened by Oliver Stanley, Minister of Transport. According to the catalogue, visitors were entertained by a "programme of music as played on the LNER Harwich–Antwerp Steamships by 'His Master's Voice' Electrical Reproducer". Several thousand visitors attended these exhibitions. Smaller displays held outside London were also very popular.

The reaction of both press and public to the posters issued by the companies was generally favourable. Advertising and publicity matters received widespread coverage in journals, including the *Railway Gazette*, and both national and provincial newspapers took an interest as well. There was little criticism, although some of the more adventurous designs commissioned by Teasdale and Dandridge caused problems. Public opinion is more difficult to judge, but what evidence there is seems to show a preference for more traditional designs. In 1928 the LMS published a list of its six best-selling posters (*Railway Gazette* 9 November). Paul Henry took the first two places with views of Connemara (page 104) and Lough Derg, followed by Maurice Greiffenhagen, Algernon Talmage, Sir D. Y. Cameron and Norman Wilkinson.

Posters did run into trouble, often from unexpected sources. In 1933 a railway engineer wrote to the *Railway Gazette* to complain about a poster recently issued by the Southern. Under the heading "Wrong Impressionist Posters" he described the design as a "throw-back" and went on: "A railway is an engineer-ing concern, without engineers it could not function for a single day. Therefore for a railway to exhibit posters, with the object of attracting passengers, depicting equipment the use of which – if it were possible to use it – would court disaster, is not good policy. It can attract only the ignorant and it invites the ridicule of all intelligent engineers – and quite a respectable proportion of the public are engineers today. Railway poster designs incorporating engineering equipment might surely be submitted to a qualified censor before being accepted for display. It is positively offensive to an engineer to be invited to travel on a railway with signals which defy the Ministry of Transport regulations, or the trains of which, however vividly coloured, are hauled by out-of-gauge locomotives whose cab, and the enginemen therein, recall pictures of Shadrach, Meshach and Abed-nego" (27 January).

This was too much even for the *Railway Gazette*. "Does not our correspondent view this poster question rather too seriously?" it asked, and a reply came in the next issue from Cuthbert Grasemann, Public Relations and Advertising Officer with the Southern: "I notice, the writer says, that incorrect impressionist posters only attract the ignorant, and as the writer of the letter must have been attracted by the posters, otherwise he would not have noticed them, I presume the category in which he places himself may account for the fact that he designates the railways as engineering concerns. There is no doubt that the railways have suffered severely by being treated as engineering concerns instead of as a simple business proposition."

Grasemann went on to emphasize the need for the poster to be noticed, in order to do its job, and he made no apology for using fashionable images if this would help. The poster had to "carry", to get the message across, and for designers like Purvis this had to be done quickly as the passenger hurried past. "The most valuable asset of a well designed poster," he told the Bradford Publicity Club on 2 February 1929, "is its shock value. By shock value I mean its kick, strength, visibility, immediate readability. In this lies the poster's greatest value to the advertiser. It is the spearhead of the charge or the shock troops of the campaign."

But not all passengers were hurrying past. Many were waiting on platforms for trains and could study posters in more detail than they might have liked. The companies were able to issue designs which in other circumstances would have been considered failures. Maps and aerial views fell into this category. They had always been popular but during this period they were developed in new and novel ways. In 1934 Montague Black produced a set of six "bird's-eye" views of the area served by the LNER from the Home Counties to Scotland (page 150). It became common to add historical information and details of places to visit. J. P. Sayer designed several maps of this kind for the Great

Western, including one of Royal Leamington Spa and its surrounding district (page 41), but one of the best came from Arthur Watts with his "Map of the Lake District" for the LMS (page 118).

SUNSHINE AND LEISURE

In an address to the Berlin Advertising Convention in 1930, Cecil Dandridge identified over fifteen principle types of poster issued by the LNER. The most numerous was "specific geographical" (*Railway Gazette* 16 May). By this he meant posters advertising holiday destinations, and it was with the seaside resort that the poster had always been most closely associated. Railways had played a vital role in the development of resorts during the nineteenth century and had provided fast access from the towns and cities. Many resorts had grown rapidly in size while others, including Skegness, were created by the arrival of their first line. The number of visitors continued to grow, in spite of the difficult economic conditions of the inter-war years, and by 1935 Blackpool alone was receiving over seven million visitors a year. The railways still carried most visitors to resorts, although they began to suffer increasing competition from motor coaches. Despite the fact that holiday traffic on the railways more than tripled during this period, their actual share of the total number of visitors decreased and this was a trend that was to continue in the future.

Many posters of resorts were issued by the companies as part of joint advertising schemes with the local authority or publicity bureau. This had advantages – it helped co-operation and shared costs, as well as eliminating wasteful competition – but it also caused problems. "Spread out on my study floor," wrote Walter Shaw Sparrow in *Advertising and British Art*, "is a largely handled poster, a very pleasing synthesis of a seaside front. Are the inhabitants of this town pleased? No. They look upon decorative art as a window-pane, or series of window-panes, and wish to see on their hoardings a tinted photograph lithographed in all details into a very bad poster." The need for designs to be approved by a local committee, often conservative in taste, led frequently to uninspired posters that made the resort appear worthy but dull. The LNER was alone

in refusing to accept this and made it clear to resort authorities that the choice of artist and style of design rested with their Advertising Manager. "Posters are placed on station boards and other property for the appearance of which he is responsible," stated Francis Goodricke, adding that this policy had proved "entirely acceptable to everyone concerned" (*Railway Gazette* 7 December 1928).

The LNER led the way in broadening the theme of the resort poster and issued a series of designs which featured beach scenes and the fun of the seaside. Beach scenes had been used in the past – one of the most memorable images of the Edwardian era, which had been issued by the Great Northern Railway, was of the "Jolly Fisherman" skipping along at Skegness – but they were not common, and most posters of resorts avoided the beach. When it was shown, it usually appeared in the distance beyond the sophisticated visitors on the promenade. This attitude persisted into the 1920s, even among resorts that had abandoned attempts to attract a more select clientele and had long since given themselves over to trippers.

Many resorts liked to appear more genteel than they actually were and disliked their reputation, despite the income it brought. "Advertising enterprise", wrote Walter Shaw Sparrow in *Advertising and British Art*, "is given to places which are delightful resorts for the cosier classes. A few weeks ago, outside King's Cross Station, three kiddies of the poor stood looking at a poster of a northern seaside, but the contrast between its well-to-do holidaying and the drab, dingy little Londoners turned the seaside into a snob. Not that there was envy in the children's remarks on the poster. 'Must be very nice there,' one of them said. 'Oh, very nice, and p'haps some day we'll go there too.' Charity may take them for a day or so to the yellow sands, or a cheap trip in a crowded train may enable them to invade that pride of custom which regards trippers at the seaside as offensive to superior families."

The "Jolly Fisherman" was an English alternative to the provocative mademoiselles common in posters on the continent. The epitome of good, clean British fun, his portly appearance and air of contentment was designed to appeal to the working man and his family (see page 149).

The LNER varied its advertising according to the nature of the resort and the type of visitor it was trying to attract. It saw no point in trying to tempt sophisticated visitors to popular resorts like Skegness, Bridlington or Mablethorpe, or trippers to Tynemouth or the Belgian Coast. In some cases, including that of Scarborough, it juggled its posters carefully to appeal to both groups. The other companies were slow to follow, although their advertising of resorts did become more adventurous during the 1930s.

In addition to posters of resorts, the companies ran more general campaigns to publicize the holiday areas that they served. The LNER again set the pace with its continual promotion of the East Coast as "The Drier Side". Posters and other publicity material were used to emphasize its delights and those of more specific areas, including the Yorkshire Coast and East Anglia, so that the actual choice of resort was not so important. The Southern also used slogans and campaigns successfully. Like the Great Western it promoted its winter climate – "South for Winter Sunshine" was used regularly – but it reserved its best efforts for the summer. "South for Sunshine" and "The Sun Shines Most on the Southern Coast" frequently appeared and the Southern reinforced this image with its use of popular characters. The little boy standing at the end of the platform made his debut in 1925 and reappeared over the years in a variety of formats, including several foreign language versions. Sunny South Sam who, according to the *Railway Gazette*, possessed the "intelligent features of a cheery and typical Southern Railway guard" (14 March 1930), first beamed out at passengers in 1930. He appeared in folders, guides and newspaper advertisements as well as posters, and specialized in presenting Meteorological Office sunshine statistics which, of course, showed the Southern well ahead.

The companies named many of their holiday trains in order to attract further publicity. The Southern was again well to the fore, not only with the *Brighton Belle* and *Bournemouth Belle*, both run in association with the Pullman Car Company, but also the *Atlantic Coast Express* which carried holiday-makers to the resorts of Devon and North Cornwall. In 1947 it introduced the *Devon Belle* with its distinctive observation car at the rear of the train. The Great Western ran several famous trains, including the *Cornish Riviera Express* which had been introduced as the *Cornish Riviera Limited* in 1904. The company celebrated the twenty-fifth anniversary of the train in 1929 by building new carriages which it described in a commemorative booklet *A Silver Anniversary – The Cornish Riviera Express, 1904–1929*. These boasted better facilities, more seating space, and also the innovation of "Vita glass, which admits those health-giving ultra-violet rays from the sun which ordinary window glass excludes." This was not only good for passengers but also enabled them to start their holiday earlier: "passengers by these new trains will literally commence their sunlight treatment en route to the holiday destination."

Although posters played an important part in publicity campaigns, they were only part of the total effort. Equally important were the guides and booklets that were produced in great numbers, especially the general handbooks issued by each company for the holiday areas it served. *Holiday Haunts* was published by the Great Western, *Hints for Holidays* by the Southern, *Holidays by LMS* by the LMS and *The Holiday Handbook* by the LNER. Each contained a series of brief descriptions of resorts, accompanied by photographs and advertisements, travel information, details of fares, and advertisements for hotels and boarding houses.

Many of the hotels listed were run by the companies themselves. The railway companies had always run their own hotels, and accommodation was usually of a high standard. The Tregenna Castle Hotel at St Ives, one of several run by the Great Western, had panoramic views over St Ives Bay together with one hundred acres of grounds. It boasted central heating as well as a nine-hole golf course and tennis, squash and badminton courts. At Morecambe the LMS completely rebuilt the Midland Hotel in 1933 to form part of a new sea wall and esplanade constructed by the local council. Designed by Oliver Hill in the modernist style, it had sculpture by Eric Gill and murals by Eric Ravilious. There were over forty bedrooms, most of which overlooked the sea and had their own private balconies.

But not everyone who visited the sea or countryside stayed in hotels and boarding houses. Many were attracted by the benefits of the open-air life, and camping grew in popularity during these years. The LNER took advantage of this trend in 1933 when it introduced the camping coach. These were specially fitted coaches and were usually located at stations and sidings. They were available for hire by parties of six at a cost of two pounds, ten shillings a week or three pounds for the larger size of coach. Linen, cooking utensils and crockery were provided. The Great Western introduced camping coaches in 1934, while the LMS began to provide what it called caravan coaches. This was also the time when the holiday camp was becoming well established. The first camp had opened in the mid-1920s and during the following decade many more were built. "Our True Intent is all for your Delight" was the Shakespearian motto of Billy Butlin who opened his first camp at Skegness in 1937 and another at Clacton in the following year. He and the LNER joined forces to advertise both camps. The LMS built its own camp in partnership with Thomas Cook. This opened at Prestatyn in 1939 but was requisitioned by the army shortly after the outbreak of the Second World War.

Inland resorts and holiday areas were promoted vigorously with posters. Spas continued to attract many

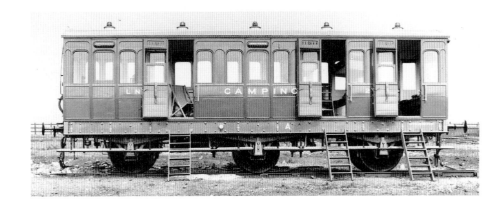

An LNER camping coach at Sandsend, near Whitby, in 1934.

visitors, and the smaller centres were not forgotten. In 1923 the Great Western and LMS joined forces with several local authorities to advertise Llandrindod Wells and the other spas of Central Wales. Many scenic areas had been made accessible by the railways, often in the face of serious opposition, and the LMS in particular served an impressive range of destinations including the Peak District, Snowdonia, the Lake District and the Scottish Highlands. These were places for healthy pursuits such as fishing, walking and climbing. Walking became extremely popular during the inter-war years and the companies, especially the Southern and LNER, published a wide range of rambling guides. The Southern organized excursions and conducted rambles, while the Great Western ran a series of Hikers' Mystery Expresses from Paddington. Other sports were promoted as well, including golf. Many fine golf courses could be reached by the LMS and LNER. Portrush was served by the LMS, while players for Silloth, home of the famous lady golfer Cecil Leitch, and the more remote course at Cruden Bay were carried by the LNER.

Architectural and historical studies were popular themes for the poster designer and were used to attract visitors to cathedrals, abbeys and other historical sites. All the companies produced posters of this type, and the work of Fred Taylor for the LNER was particularly good. The LNER also published a range of designs featuring historical events, including work by both Anna and Doris Zinkeisen, and a set of three "battle" posters by Frank Mason which appeared in 1931. Much of this style of advertising appealed to overseas visitors, particularly from the USA and Canada, and the companies produced posters and guide books specifically for use abroad. In *Notes for American Visitors* the LNER stressed the connections of the area it served with such historical figures as the Pilgrim Fathers, George Washington and William Penn, while the Great Western, which styled itself "the holiday line of England", provided descriptions of Oxford, Windsor and Stratford-upon-Avon. London was promoted by all four companies in a variety of ways with the emphasis ranging from its tourist attractions to shopping and the lively night-life.

Posters were also used to advertise sporting and other special events. The railway companies had always run excursion trains to sporting events, particularly to football matches and race meetings, but they only issued posters for these on major occasions. Handbills and notices, which often contained a stock view to which details were added, were normally used together with press advertisements.

There were exceptions, however. Posters were published for the Olympic Games of 1928, as well as for several of the new spectator sports of the period, including greyhound and motor racing. The companies advertised exhibitions – although again rarely with posters – and often took the opportunity to advertise themselves and their services as well. They also promoted more unusual events, including the total eclipse of the sun which occurred in June 1927, and many events that they organized themselves, particularly centenary and other celebrations.

SHIPS, FREIGHT AND SPEED

Another subject of advertising by the railways in this period was transport by sea. All four companies were major owners of docks and ships. They carried both freight and passengers and provided services to Ireland (Great Western and LMS), the Channel Islands (Great Western and Southern) and the Isle of Man (LMS), as well as to the Continent. The fleets had been built up largely during the second half of the nineteenth century, and in 1923 the new companies took over, not just a large number of vessels, but also ports and services that had often been in competition with each other. The LMS owned almost seventy ships, together with an extensive network of docks, including facilities at Tilbury and Goole. It devoted a great deal of publicity to shipping subjects, partly due to the influence of Norman Wilkinson.

Some of the finest advertising was produced by the LNER and the Southern in promoting their routes to the Continent. The LNER operated from several ports, including Hull and Grimsby, but its main passenger service was from Harwich to the Hook of Holland, Flushing and Zeebrugge. This was the established route to Germany and Central Europe and enabled the LNER to produce posters for a variety of destinations including Munich, Budapest and Prague, as well as Holland and the Belgian Coast. It also issued many fine studies by Frank Mason of vessels at work including "Three New Ships" (page 139) which appeared in 1930. These were the *S S Vienna*, which was introduced in 1929, and the *S S Prague* and *S S Amsterdam* which followed the next year.

Other publicity material produced by the LNER included newspaper advertisements and a book of verses with the title *Ludicrous Limericks*. This featured a series of travellers wishing to reach destinations via Harwich, such as Utrecht:

Said a certain young man: "I expect
Very shortly to go to Utrecht."
When they asked: "Where is that?"
He exclaimed: "Oh my hat!
Did you suffer from early neglect?"

Let us hope there are not many so ignorant – The Netherlands via Harwich. (*London & North Eastern Railway Magazine*, September 1939)

"Southern for the Continent" was the slogan regularly used by the Southern which operated services from Dover, Folkestone, Newhaven and Southampton. This was still a time when air competition was not a serious threat, and its routes, particularly those from Dover and Folkestone, were heavily used. They provided the shortest crossings of the Channel – a fact which the Southern was not slow to exploit. In its guide *The Peerless Riviera* it promoted the route from Dover to Calais as both the quickest and the most fashionable. "With all simplicity and lack of exertion and fatigue it has transformed the erstwhile tediousness of travel into a veritable pleasure. It is the route of Diplomacy, Fashion, Sport, Business, the Stage, the Arts. This is the way Kings and Princes pass. It is the Great Highway to the Continent." On arrival at Calais passengers were able to join the *Calais–Mediterranean Express* or *Through Riviera Rapide* which would be waiting to whisk them away to the south.

The Southern carried through a series of improvements during these years. In 1929 it introduced the *S S Canterbury* which was initially for the exclusive use of passengers on the *Golden Arrow Pullman* service from London to Paris. This was followed two years later by the appearance of its first car-ferry. In 1936, in association with the Chemin de Fer du Nord and the ALA Steamship Company, it opened a new train-ferry service between Dover and Dunkirk which was mainly for freight but also carried a nightly sleeping-car service. The company also continued to develop Southampton as a major port, and improved facilities were provided for both freight vessels and liners. The liner trade had been moving away from Liverpool and other ports for many years, and these improvements, which included the opening of the King George V Graving Dock in 1933, continued the trend.

Freight was an important source of revenue for the railways but was not a subject that produced outstanding advertising. The companies carried an enormous range of goods, from the coal and steel of heavy industry to food and perishable items and house, farm and factory removals. It was an area in which they faced considerable problems during this period, caused not only by the economic depression, which had a particularly serious effect on the LNER, but also by intense competition from road transport. They responded in a number of ways. There was investment in new facilities, including the modernization of goods depots, increased use of containers, and provision of faster and more regular services. Attempts were made to attract new

Crossing the Channel in style. The dining saloon of the *SS Canterbury* awaits passengers from the *Golden Arrow* c. 1929.

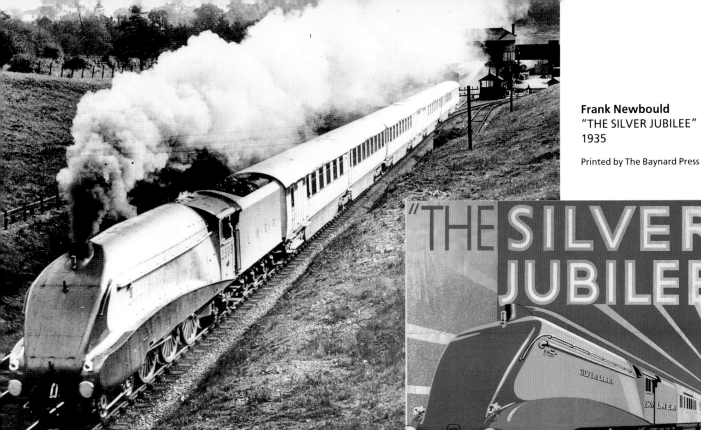

The Silver Jubilee at Hadley Wood, near New Barnet, in September 1935.

Frank Newbould
"THE SILVER JUBILEE"
1935

Printed by The Baynard Press

industry by making land available for development alongside the line, although these were only partially successful and most new factories were built with no railway connection.

Joint advertising between all four companies was also adopted. In 1935 a campaign was launched to advertise the range of facilities that were offered, such as rail-road containers, warehousing, registered transit, country lorry services, special wagons and household removals. Posters, folders and magazine advertising were used extensively, and further campaigns followed in later years. In 1938 the companies combined to mount the Square Deal campaign. This was an attempt to persuade the Government to remove the remaining restrictions on the railway companies, especially over the regulation of rates and charges, so that they could compete on equal terms with the road haulage industry. It was given a high profile and, in addition to the usual range of publicity material, there was a great deal of press coverage and banners were draped outside stations and across bridges.

Some of the best advertising of these years was used to promote prestige trains and services. Many of the former companies had stressed the speed and comfort of their trains, particularly those that operated the routes between London and Scotland. This rivalry was continued by the LMS and LNER during the 1920s. Both the *Royal Scot* of the LMS and *Flying Scotsman* of the LNER ran non-stop to Scotland but they did not compete on speed; it was not until the following decade that the pace began to quicken. In 1935 the LNER introduced its first streamlined train, the *Silver Jubilee*, which ran between London and Newcastle. This was followed two years later by the *Coronation* which covered the distance between London and Edinburgh in only six hours. The LMS hit back with the *Coronation Scot* which took an extra thirty minutes between London and Glasgow.

These trains, with their own locomotives and carriages, were highly distinctive and extremely popular. They generated an enormous amount of publicity material, including many posters. Frank Mason, Tom Purvis and Doris Zinkeisen all produced designs for the *Coronation*, while the *Coronation Scot* featured in posters by Bryan de Grineau (page 117) and Norman Wilkinson. A fine study of *Coronation* class locomotives under construction at the LMS Works at Crewe was also contributed by Lili Réthi (page 117). Although speed was important it was not seen as the only way of attracting passengers, and both the LMS and LNER emphasized the standard of comfort and facilities available on these and other trains. The *Flying Scotsman* boasted a hairdressing saloon, ladies' resting room, Louis XVI restaurant and cocktail bar and even a cinema coach for a short period. Several posters were issued by the LNER to advertise its restaurant car and dining facilities, including work by Tom Purvis and A. R. Thomson, as well as the "Chef and Waiter" series by Austin Cooper (page 143).

But, despite the work of the poster artists, the image of the streamlined train and the serving of delicious meals and crusted port was far from reality for most passengers. Railway catering was generally experienced in the station refreshment room. This had always had a bad reputation and in 1923, when the *Birmingham Mail* reported an important archaeological discovery, things had clearly not changed. "Poultry 3,000 years old has been discovered in the tomb of Tutankhamen," it noted. "We understand that tenders for the whole consignment have already been received from various railway refreshment room contractors" (*Great Western Railway Magazine* May 1923).

Travelling was often no better. In 1930 the LNER capitalized on the success of J. B. Priestley's *The Good Companions* by having the theatre company photographed at Marylebone on their way to Manchester. It went on to publish posters by Austin Cooper and Tom Purvis with the slogan "We Carried the Good Companions – Now let us Carry You". But when Priestley embarked on his *English Journey* in the autumn of 1933 to see the new England of the suburb and arterial road, he travelled by motor coach. He rarely ventured on to the train but when he did, as between Hull and Lincoln, he experienced a journey far from the image that the LNER Advertising Department was trying to project: "A short but somewhat complicated train journey took me to Lincoln. Fog descended upon the brief afternoon; and there were patterns of frost everywhere. I stamped my feet on deserted station platforms, under dim lights; I travelled in old and empty carriages, which rumbled into the dark plain of Lincolnshire; and I peered through the misted windows at mysterious little stations. It was not a journey in this year, this life. I felt like a family solicitor in a mid Victorian novel, something by Wilkie Collins or Charles Reade; probably going to some remote Grange to read a tortuous and sinister will" (*English Journey* 1934).

"Is Your Journey Really Necessary?" (c. 1943) was designed by Bert Thomas for the Railway Executive Committee.

THE FINAL YEARS

The outbreak of the Second World War in September 1939 saw the hoardings cleared of most advertising material. Space was created for posters and notices issued by the newly formed Railway Executive Committee, who had become responsible for running the network, and for giving information on urgent matters, including emergency timetables, air-raid warnings and reduced facilities. However, many posters of resorts did remain, partly to brighten up stations, and the Committee agreed to allow the joint advertising schemes between the resorts and railway companies to continue during 1940. Posters were issued for the new season, as were holiday guides and handbooks. These were slimmer than in previous years, and there was much emphasis on those parts of the coast declared safe areas by the Government, but the tone was defiant. At Eastbourne "a wonderful range of attractions both in summer and winter are offered to visitors and residents alike," declared *Hints for Holidays*, "and 'business as usual' is the town's motto for 1940."

As late as May, the *Railway Gazette* was able to report that the joint schemes were continuing, despite paper shortages, but the tone soon changed as the war came closer to home. Travel was discouraged. "Is Your Journey Really Necessary?" and "The Signal is Against Holiday Travel" became common slogans. They alternated with more subtle messages emphasizing the contribution that the railways were making to the war effort and the fact that "Food, Shells and Fuel *Must* Come First". Nevertheless, travel was not prohibited, and most resorts remained open. Holiday-makers continued to find their way to the coast, although they received no encouragement and often had to endure journeys that were long and uncomfortable.

The end of the war in Europe in 1945 saw the election of a government committed to the nationalization of the railway network, but it was not in a position to put its plans into immediate effect. Recovery was slow as economic problems and the serious work of reconstruction created a climate that was not conducive to holidays. Gradually conditions improved. "John Citizen has time to look about him once again," announced *Hints for Holidays* on its reappearance in 1947, "and now he is eager to rediscover his England, to roam its green countryside, to lie on its now unmenaced beaches, to stroll through the streets of its ancient cities, of which so much loveliness has escaped the desolation of war."

The Southern produced several impressive posters during its final two years. These included work by Walter Spradbery and Norman Wilkinson, as well as two fascinating studies by Helen McKie of Waterloo in war and post-war guise which were commissioned for the centenary celebrations of the opening of the station (page 91). The LMS continued its policy of showing the day-to-day work of the railway and commissioned designs from Septimus Scott and Terence Cuneo. Cuneo, who was later to produce a series of designs for British Railways, was also commissioned by the LNER to design a poster showing locomotives at Doncaster Works, and towards the end of 1947 the company issued "East Coast Occupations", a set of four posters by Frank Mason (page 152).

Posters published by the Great Western during this period included views of London and Plymouth by Frank Mason and Frank Newbould (pages 54–6) which showed none of the destruction that the two cities had suffered. Newbould did, however, reflect the determination to rebuild the city in the title of his poster – "The Spirit of Drake Lives On" – and the destruction was also mentioned in *Hints for Holidays* which maintained an optimistic note: "Not much remains of the town's earlier buildings; a wave of Victorian 'improvement' saw to that; then, in their turn, many of the later buildings vanished during air raids. Yet, in spite of its scars, Plymouth has much to offer that is interesting."

In 1947 the Great Western published *Next Station* by Christian Barman, outlining its ambitious plans for the future, but by this time the company was in its final year. With the creation of the British Transport Commission on 1 January 1948 the companies passed into public ownership. The network came under the control of the Railway Executive, although for day-to-day operation it was divided into regions. The regions corresponded roughly to the areas covered by the four companies, with the major exceptions being that Scotland formed a region of its own, while the LNER in England was split into two. Public ownership brought optimism and hope to many, and this was reflected in several of the early posters that were produced. It was not long before the holiday poster made a welcome return. During the 1950s and 1960s it recaptured much of the fun of its earlier years, and passengers again found it difficult to resist the lure of coast and countryside. The only problem was that fewer of them were travelling by train. The railway was no longer the only way to go, and for more and more people it was not the way to go at all.

TRAINS OF OUR TIMES

BRITISH RAILWAYS

Three types of motive power in use on British Railways and four of the new standard locomotive and rolling stock liveries are exemplified in this scene near Bushey in the London Midland Region, at the point where water-troughs are provided on the up and down main lines. On the left is a Class 5 4-6-0 mixed traffic steam locomotive, finished black, lined in red cream and grey. In the centre is the twin diesel-electric locomotive unit Nos. 10000-10001 in black and silver hauling a main line train of carmine and cream coaches, and on the right is a suburban electric train in the malachite green livery.

BRITISH RAILWAYS

The brave new world of British Railways: steam, diesel and electric trains in a poster by Victor Welch (1949).

Artist unknown
THE SHORTEST ROUTE BETWEEN
LONDON AND BIRMINGHAM IS
BY GWR
1924

This poster was designed by the printers in GWR Windsor brown and white (chocolate and cream). The information is projected boldly at the onlooker. The same format was used again in the 1930s. The coat of arms is the Great Western emblem, comprising the crests of London and Bristol, the two cities that the company was formed to link. This emblem changed slightly over the years but remained in use until 1948, long after the Great Western had spread to serve other major centres.

Printed by Philip Reid, 47 Fleet Street, London EC4

Louis Burleigh Bruhl
FALMOUTH
1927

Printed by David Allen & Sons Ltd, London

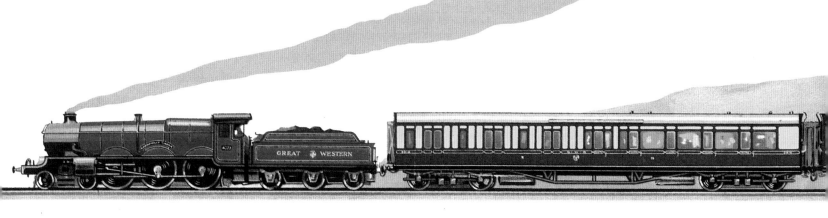

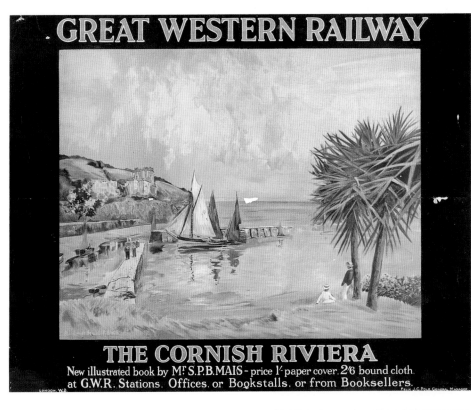

GREAT WESTERN RAILWAY

THE CORNISH RIVIERA

New illustrated book by Mr S.P.B.MAIS - price 1/ paper cover. 2'6 bound cloth. at G.W.R. Stations, Offices, or Bookstalls, or from Booksellers.

Louis Burleigh Bruhl
THE CORNISH RIVIERA
c. 1925

The Great Western likened the Cornish Riviera, with its azure sea, superb coastline, sandy bays and picturesque harbours, to the Mediterranean. Cornwall was promoted as the warmest place in Britain and also as a land of legend, superstition and romance, the home of the wild and imaginative.

F. J. Widgery
GLORIOUS DEVON
1925

The treatment of light, shade and distance in this poster is particularly striking. Glorious Devon was blessed with the amenities of the seaside and beautiful scenery in both its coast and moors. The guide *Rambles and Walking Tours in South Devon* pointed out that although a Devon mile was no longer than any other mile, a hilly walk would work out longer than a flat one as distances were measured on a flat map. Thus, as Devon was nearly all hills, the rambles would be longer than stated and more strenuous than usual! Rambling and hiking were popular pastimes in the 1920s and 1930s. Travellers were encouraged to catch the Hiker's Mystery Express at Paddington and "join the great adventure". Easter holiday snack boxes could be bought for a shilling in 1932.

Printed by S.P. & Co.

G·W·R

GLORIOUS DEVON

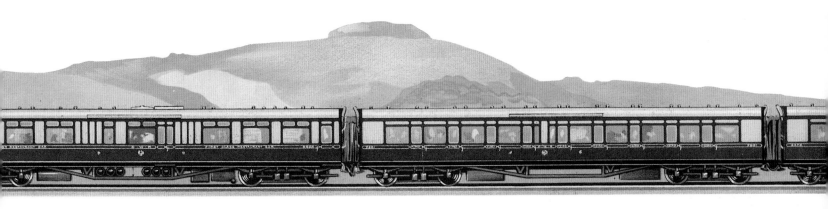

W. E. Leadley
MARLBOROUGH FOR DOWNS &
FOREST
1927

Printed by John Waddington Ltd, Leeds & London

Bruce Angrave
SOUTH WALES
c. 1928

This poster was produced in
conjunction with the South Wales
coastal resorts. The Great Western
favoured this approach to cut costs
and increase the circulation of its
publicity material. However, it could
also result in predictable posters that
lacked inspiration. Here the bracing air
tactic is laboured. Bracing air was
considered to be good for the
constitution and was used innovatively
much earlier by the Great Northern
Railway in its posters of Skegness.

Printed by Garamond Press Ltd, London

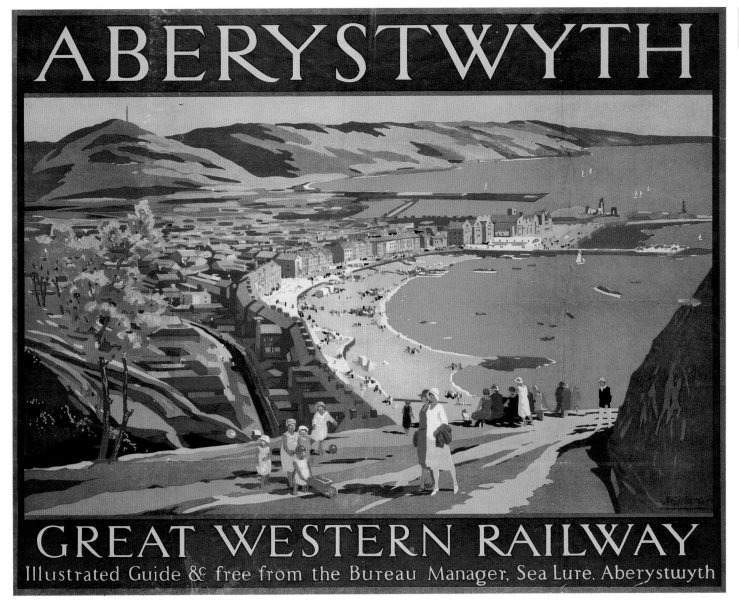

A. E. Martin
ABERYSTWYTH
1928

Aberystwyth was presented as a
bustling, crowded, sunny seaside town
for the fashionable set.

Printed by Dangerfield Printing Co. Ltd, London

Artist unknown
TORQUAY
1927

Torquay was promoted as the capital
of the "English Riviera". It faces south
and is situated on thickly wooded
slopes. During the winter the air is so
mild that sub-tropical plants continue
to thrive in the open air – hence the
palm tree.

Printed by Philip Reid, 47 Fleet Street, London EC4

W. Russell Flint
CHESTER
c. 1930

Printed by Bemrose & Sons Ltd

GLORIOUS SOUTH DEVON
1928

This poster was reproduced from a photograph that appeared in *The Times*. The *Torbay Express* left Paddington at noon, arriving in Torquay at 3.30 p.m. It then continued to Paignton and Kingswear where passengers could cross by ferry to Dartmouth.

Printed by Sun Engraving Co. Ltd, London & Watford

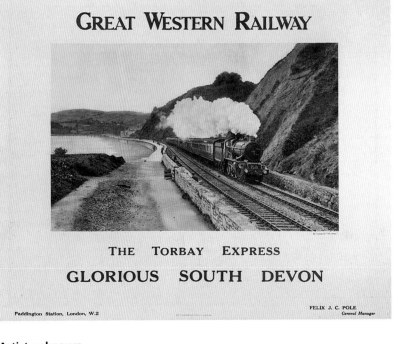

Artist unknown
CARDIFF – THE CITY OF CONFERENCES
1932

Cardiff was a major port for the export of coal. The Great Western served its coalfields and promoted its commercial potentialities.

Printed by Western Mail & Echo Ltd, Cardiff

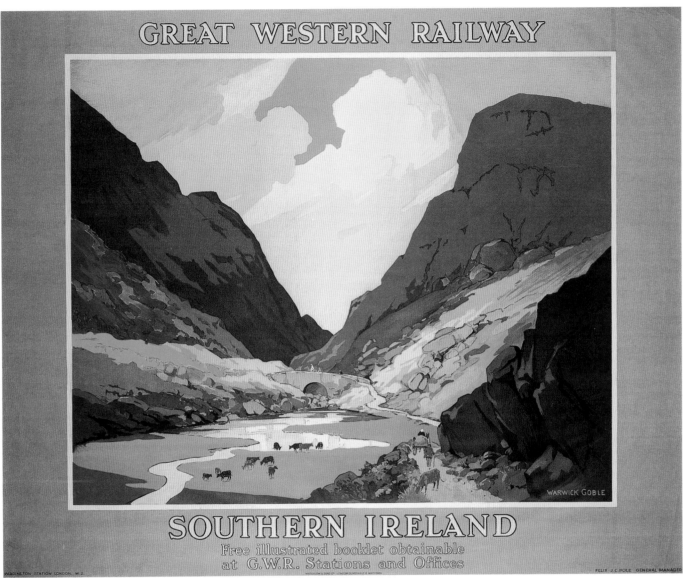

GREAT WESTERN RAILWAY

SOUTHERN IRELAND

Free illustrated booklet obtainable
at G.W.R. Stations and Offices

Freda Lingstrom
TINTERN ABBEY
1931

Two hundred of these posters were printed and sent for display in the USA. The version used in Britain omitted the word "England". In 1927 the Great Western had broken new ground by introducing "Land Cruises", aimed at the overseas as well as the home visitor. Tickets were offered for holiday tours very much like the package holidays of today. The scheme included first-class travel by rail and road, meals and accommodation, and first-class hotels. The Wye Valley was one of the first to be offered, together with Shakespeare Country, and these were later followed by the Marlborough Downs, Cheddar Valley and Cotswold Hills. The intention was to "make haste slowly": progress was leisurely; long, fatiguing road journeys were avoided. These "Land Cruises" continued for many years. Other tours and excursions on offer included the novel monthly return ticket, day tour, half-day excursion and cheap day ticket.

Printed by J. Weiner Ltd, London WC1

Warwick Goble
SOUTHERN IRELAND
c. 1931

This poster gives the potential traveller an impression of the space and timelessness of Southern Ireland. It was also available as a jigsaw puzzle containing 150 pieces and costing two shillings and sixpence.

Printed by Waterlow & Sons Ltd, London, Dunstable & Watford

THE BOY KING HENRY III CROWNED
GLOUCESTER CATHEDRAL 28 OCT. 1216

GWR GLOUCESTER LMS
CATHEDRAL

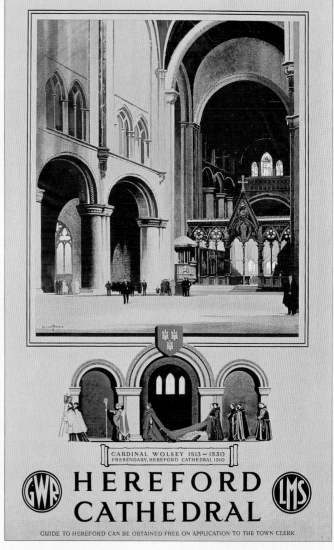

CARDINAL WOLSEY 1513 – 1530
PREBENDARY, HEREFORD CATHEDRAL 1510

GWR HEREFORD LMS
CATHEDRAL

GUIDE TO HEREFORD CAN BE OBTAINED FREE ON APPLICATION TO THE TOWN CLERK

Claude Buckle
GLOUCESTER CATHEDRAL
c. 1933

Printed by Beck & Inchbold Ltd, Leeds, London &
Glasgow

Claude Buckle
HEREFORD CATHEDRAL
c. 1933

Printed by McCorquodale & Co. Ltd, London

Claude Buckle
WORCESTER CATHEDRAL
c. 1933

Printed by Jordison & Co., London &
Middlesbrough

Three posters produced jointly by the
Great Western and the LMS.
Cathedrals, abbeys and castles along
the line were widely advertised in
posters, guides and books. Travellers
were encouraged to see every
cathedral in England. The cathedral
guides, published by the Great
Western, were well researched and
historically accurate, and were far
more academic and detailed than
many issued today.

Leslie Carr
EXETER
c. 1931

Printed by Waterlow & Sons Ltd, London,
Dunstable & Watford

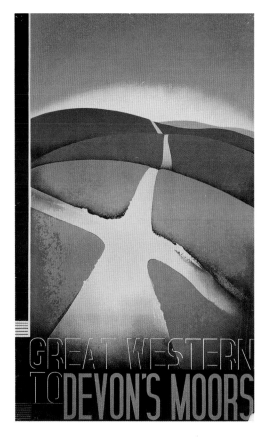

Edward McKnight Kauffer
GREAT WESTERN TO DEVON'S MOORS
1933

Edward McKnight Kauffer
GO GREAT WESTERN TO CORNWALL
1933

Printed by William Brown & Co. Ltd, London EC3

Two posters from a series of six featuring Devon and Cornwall. Kauffer was one of the many artists influenced by the new European art movements of the early twentieth century and had established his reputation with his work for London Transport. His designs made great use of geometrical pattern. 2,000 copies of each poster in the series were printed.

J. P. Sayer
ROYAL LEAMINGTON SPA
1933

The Oak Tree of Leamington (or Midland Oak) was said to mark the centre of England, although several other oak trees in the Midlands also lay claim to this honour. The tree was seriously damaged in a gale and, as it was also badly decayed, was cut down by the local council in 1967. It is said to have been 1,000 years old. The acorns were kept by the Parks Department and a sapling planted a hundred yards away from the original site as the old tree was considered to be a traffic hazard.

Printed by W.E. Berry Ltd, Bradford

Ralph & Brown
GWR AIR SERVICES
1933
Original artwork

The Great Western took the lead in getting the railways off the ground. The first Great Western air service was between Cardiff and Plymouth. In 1933 Imperial Airways supplied the plane, crew and engineers, and the Great Western supplied the traffic staff. The plane itself was a Westland Wessex monoplane, painted in the Great Western colours of Windsor brown and white (chocolate and cream), with the company badge on each side of the rudder. When the plane landed at Plymouth the passengers were transferred to a bus which connected the airport with the railway station. The cost from Cardiff to Plymouth was three pounds, ten shillings single and six pounds return. Letters were also carried on the service for three pence above the normal postal rate. The first season resulted in a net loss, so in 1934 a plan was drawn up to establish an airline jointly owned by the four major railway companies and Imperial Airways. This became known as Railway Air Services and continued until 1939 when the Government claimed their services for the war effort. Operations eventually ground to a halt in 1947.

Dora Batty
HISTORIC BATH
1935

Bath was promoted for the curative qualities of its waters, as well as its unique historic interest and Georgian architecture. The Great Western emphasized the reputation of Bath as the "English Athens" of the eighteenth century and a centre of art, literature and fashion. Dora Batty produced several other posters for the Great Western and also designed posters for London Transport.

Printed by Lowe & Brydone Printers Ltd, London

Artist unknown
COPIES OF PICTORIAL POSTERS
c. 1934

The GWR sold copies of its more popular posters; this is the reason why many survive today. This poster was probably designed by Ralph & Brown.

Printed by Jarrold & Sons Ltd, Norwich & London

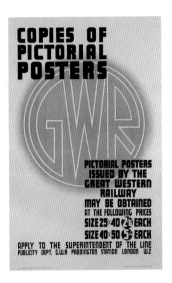

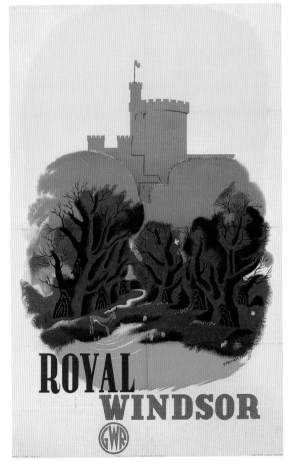

Edward McKnight Kauffer
ROYAL WINDSOR
1935

This was an ambitious poster for the Great Western. Windsor was often advertised using "fairy tale" imagery, intended to appeal largely to overseas visitors, but here they commissioned McKnight Kauffer to produce a more adventurous design. He was paid eighty-eight pounds, ten shillings.

Printed by J. Weiner Ltd, London WC1

Ronald Lampitt
CORNWALL
1936

Ronald Lampitt
DEVON
1936

These posters form part of a series of three designed by Ronald Lampitt in an innovative mosaic style using grouped rectangles in different colours. Lampitt was paid the unusually high sum of almost £200 for each design. 1,200 copies each of the "Cornwall" and "Devon" posters were printed, and 1,500 of the third, entitled "The Cotswold Country". The designs were much admired. The *Railway Gazette* was particularly impressed: "The richness of colour and design obtained by the Romans in their tesselated pavements have inspired a new style of Great Western railway poster....The tesselated principle offers new possibilities in poster advertising by reason of its effectiveness when viewed from a distance" (15 May 1936). Unfortunately, the mosaic style did not catch on.

Printed by J. Weiner Ltd, London WC1

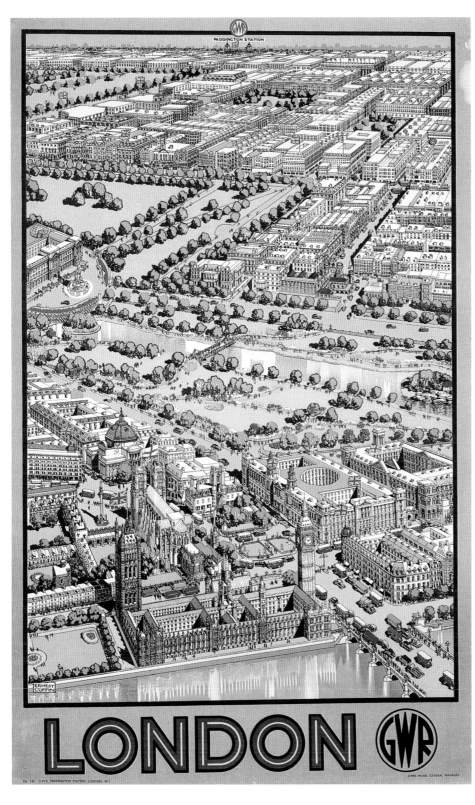

Ernest Coffin
LONDON
1936

One of a pair of posters showing London. The only named building is Paddington Station!

Ernest Coffin
OXFORD
1938

This poster was issued jointly by the Great Western and the LMS. Tom Tower in Christ Church was chosen to symbolize the importance of Oxford as a place of learning. The Great Western promoted Oxford as the City of Spires.

Printed by Beck & Inchbold Ltd, Leeds

LONDON

ENQUIRE FOR CHEAP TICKET FACILITIES

Frank Mason

LONDON – THE TOWER OF LONDON

1938

The Dangerfield Printing Co. Ltd, London

H. Alker Tripp
WALES – CADER IDRIS & THE AFON
MAWDDACH
1937

Printed by Lowe & Brydone Printers Ltd, London
NW10

G. Baker
SOUTHERN IRELAND
1937

This was accompanied by a similar
design of Wales.

Printed by Stafford & Co. Ltd, Netherfield,
Nottingham; & London

Leonard Richmond
KILLARNEY
1938

This is the version published in Britain.
It was displayed in the USA with the
words "information available from
Associated British and Irish Railways
Inc. New York" added. The American
version also states that Killarney is in
Southern Ireland.

Printed by Lowe & Brydone Printers Ltd, London
NW10

Alfred Lambart
NEWQUAY
1937

In *The Winter Resorts of the West Country*, published by the Great Western in 1925, Newquay claimed a climate of "phenomenal dryness". It also boasted the highest class of modern hotel accommodation, the best golf course and exceptionally exhilarating air. The Great Western had always encouraged holidays at home and continued to do so in the 1930s. In its poster "Wise Spending" it reminded holiday-makers that every pound spent on travelling to, and staying at, British holiday resorts helped to improve trade and relieve unemployment. A holiday in Britain was not only healthy and pleasurable but also increased the country's prosperity.

Printed by Dangerfield Printing Co. Ltd, London

Charles Pears
THE CAMBRIAN COAST
1938

The Great Western enthusiastically promoted the magnificent scenery and charm of Wales. In *Rambles around the Cambrian Coast*, published by the Great Western in 1936, Hugh Page described almost 300 miles of rambles and walks over the hills and through the valleys of the west coast of Wales. He also included a glossary of the more important Welsh geographical words.

Printed by Lowe & Brydone Printers Ltd, London NW10

Muriel Gill
THE GUIDE TO HAPPY HOLIDAYS
1939

The *Holiday Haunts* handbook was first published in 1906 and the Great Western used it year after year to publicize its resorts and services. It also advertised hotels and boarding houses. In 1906 it was priced at one penny but the cost had increased to sixpence by 1939. The booklets were also spiced with advertisements such as those for Wheatley's Stym, a "non-intoxicating alcohol", and Mazawattee tea "in sealed packets". Later, hotels, farmhouses and country lodgings were listed and graded with comments on such things as their stabling facilities, distance from the sea and cost. Letterpress posters were issued to encourage advertisers to use *Holiday Haunts* to promote their products. This was another way of subsidizing Great Western publicity.

Printed by J. Weiner Ltd, London WC1

Leonard Cusden
CLEVEDON – THE GEM OF SUNNY SOMERSET
1939

Leonard Cusden received £86 for designing this poster, and 1,500 were produced.

Printed by Stafford & Co. Ltd, Netherfield, Nottingham

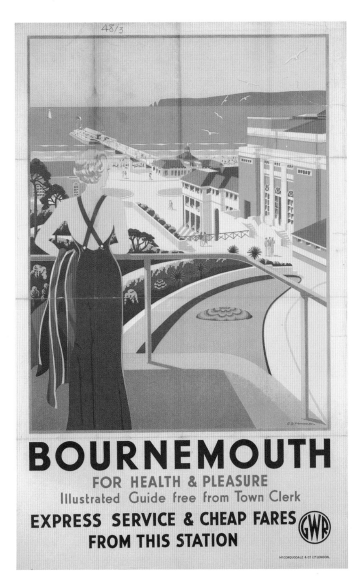

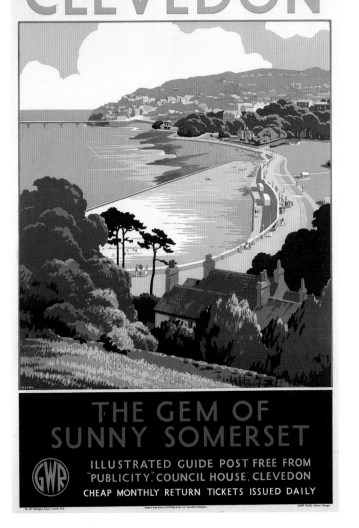

G. D. Tidmarsh
BOURNEMOUTH FOR HEALTH & PLEASURE
c. 1937

Printed by McCorquodale & Co. Ltd, London

100 YEARS OF PROGRESS
1835 — 1935

GWR

GWR **SPEED TO THE WEST** GWR
CORNWALL DEVON SOMERSET WALES

Murray Secretan
100 YEARS OF PROGRESS, 1835–1935
1935

Published to mark the centenary of the birth of the Great Western, this poster shows "King" class locomotive *King Charles II* on an express between Dawlish and Teignmouth in south Devon. In the bottom left-hand corner of the poster is a drawing of the famous Great Western broad gauge locomotive *North Star*. *North Star* was built by Robert Stephenson and Company in 1837 and was regarded as the most powerful and reliable of the early Great Western engines. A replica was built for the celebrations. The poster was designed to emphasize, not only the progress that the Great Western had made, but also its tradition of speed and reliability.

Printed by J. Weiner Ltd, London WC1

Charles Mayo
SPEED TO THE WEST
1939

In the late 1930s the steam locomotive was in its heyday, and it was the ambition of every boy to be an engine driver. This poster by Charles Mayo, who worked in the Publicity Department of the Great Western, shows a "King" class locomotive on a holiday train for the West Country. The Great Western published a book about these locomotives with the title *The "King" of Railway Locomotives*. It was the fourth volume in a series "for boys of all ages" and, like the others, was the work of W.G. Chapman. Chapman began with a quotation from the *New York Herald Tribune*: "Somewhere in the breast of every normal homo sapiens there stretches a chord which vibrates only to the sight of a fine locomotive. Even now, with airplanes and motors to bid against it in its own field of romantic interest, the steam locomotive retains its fascination." The poster was published for display in the USA with the words "The Great Western Railway of England" added, and the names of the counties omitted. It was reprinted in 1946 without the black line at the bottom.

Printed by Jordison & Co. Ltd, London & Middlesbrough

Claude Buckle
PLYMOUTH, DEVON
1938

This poster was issued jointly by the Great Western, Southern and the local council. The two companies each paid 25 per cent of the cost, and the council the remainder.

Ronald Lampitt
TENBY FOR SUNSHINE AND UNRIVALLED GOLDEN SANDS
1945

Tenby paid 75 per cent of the cost of this poster to promote its North Beach.

Printed by Jordison & Co. Ltd, London & Middlesbrough

Frank Newbould
LONDON – HEART OF THE EMPIRE
1939

Printed by Lowe & Brydone Printers Ltd, London

Frank Mason
LONDON, ST PAUL'S
1946

Frank Mason's posters of London not only capture the hustle and bustle of city activity, but also remind the viewer of the grandeur of Westminster and St Paul's. In 1946 London had survived the Second World War and looked forward to the future with hope. The posters do not depict the damage of the Blitz, but instead show life going on as normal. Mason was well known for his shipping and river scenes.

Printed by W.M. Brown & Co. Ltd, London

Frank Mason
LONDON PRIDE
1946

Printed by Haycock Press Ltd, Camberwell, London SE5

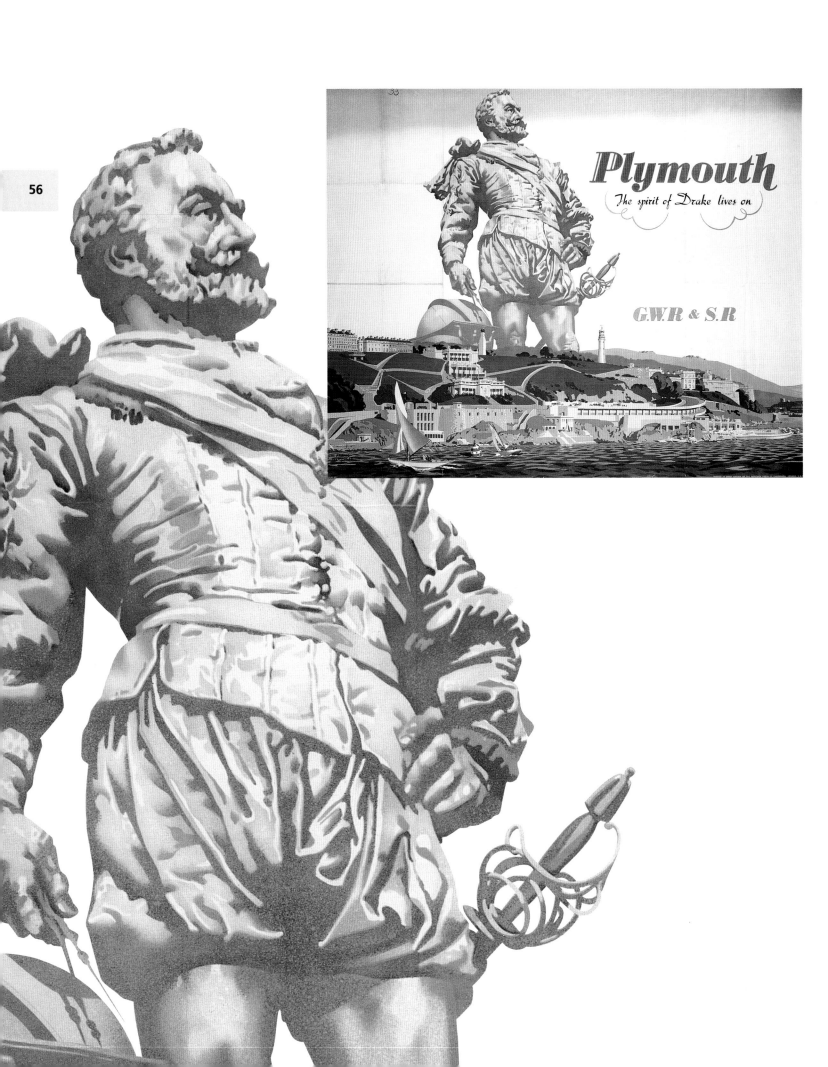

Plymouth
The spirit of Drake lives on

G.W.R & S.R

Frank Newbould
PLYMOUTH
1946

Printed by Haycock Press Ltd, Camberwell, London
SE5

Frank Newbould
SOUTH DEVON
1946

Printed by Waterlow & Sons Ltd, London &
Dunstable

Frank Newbould
THE WYE VALLEY
1946

Printed by Jordison & Co. Ltd, London &
Middlesbrough

These three posters were
commissioned from Frank Newbould
in 1946. Two were joint issues with the
Southern, including "Plymouth".
Plymouth boasted connections with
several historical and naval figures in
addition to Sir Francis Drake. Drake
would have been a popular patriotic
figure at this time. The view of the
Wye Valley was particularly successful
and was reprinted in 1947.

Artist unknown
GREAT WESTERN ROYAL HOTEL,
PADDINGTON, LONDON
c. 1939

Artist unknown
TREGENNA CASTLE HOTEL, ST IVES,
CORNWALL
c. 1939

Two posters in a series which also
included the Manor House Hotel at
Moretonhamstead, Devon, and the
Fishguard Bay Hotel. Major
improvements carried out in 1933
made the Great Western Royal Hotel
one of the most modern and
convenient in London.

Printed by Haycock Press Ltd, London SE5

Claude Buckle
WESTON SUPER-MARE
1947

A poster produced jointly by the Great
Western and the LMS. "Smiling
Somerset" was a slogan used by the
Great Western, not only for the resorts
of the coast but the county generally.
Somerset was advertised as a land of
pleasant valleys, sprinkled with old-
world villages and blessed with a
happy, comfortable atmosphere.

Printed by The Baynard Press

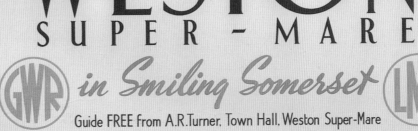

Artist unknown
DORSET COAST
1923

An early Southern Railway (South Western Section) poster in an old-fashioned style reminiscent of the former era. The new advertising policy of the Southern had yet to make an impact when this poster was produced. The Southern provided access to Dorset and the west by express restaurant-car trains.

Printed by Waterlow & Sons Ltd, London, Dunstable & Watford

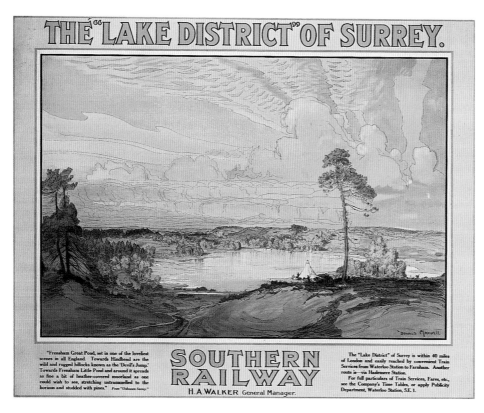

Donald Maxwell
THE "LAKE DISTRICT" OF SURREY
1924

This shows a view of Frensham Lakes. Other posters in the series of county views include the Weald of Kent, North Cornwall and the Valley of the Arun.

Printed by McCorquodale & Co. Ltd, London

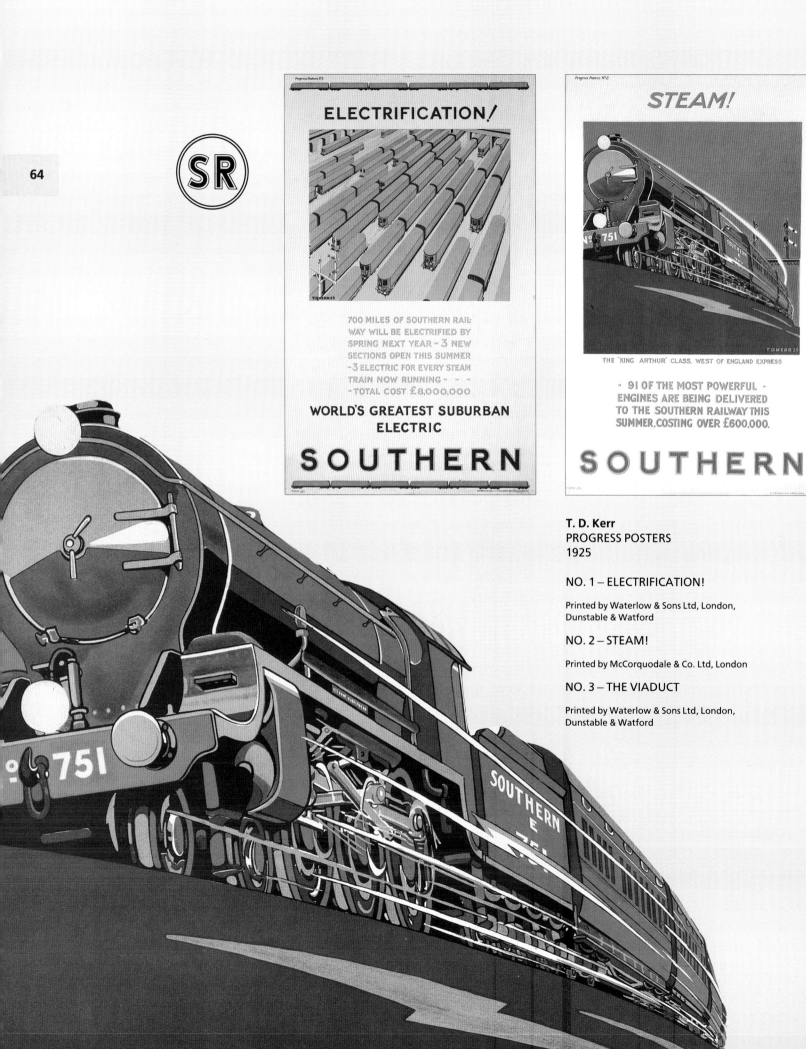

ELECTRIFICATION!

700 MILES OF SOUTHERN RAIL-
WAY WILL BE ELECTRIFIED BY
SPRING NEXT YEAR ~ 3 NEW
SECTIONS OPEN THIS SUMMER
~ 3 ELECTRIC FOR EVERY STEAM
TRAIN NOW RUNNING ~ - ~
~ TOTAL COST £8,000,000

WORLD'S GREATEST SUBURBAN
ELECTRIC

SOUTHERN

STEAM!

THE "KING ARTHUR" CLASS, WEST OF ENGLAND EXPRESS

~ 91 OF THE MOST POWERFUL ~
ENGINES ARE BEING DELIVERED
TO THE SOUTHERN RAILWAY THIS
SUMMER, COSTING OVER £600,000.

SOUTHERN

T. D. Kerr
PROGRESS POSTERS
1925

NO. 1 – ELECTRIFICATION!

Printed by Waterlow & Sons Ltd, London,
Dunstable & Watford

NO. 2 – STEAM!

Printed by McCorquodale & Co. Ltd, London

NO. 3 – THE VIADUCT

Printed by Waterlow & Sons Ltd, London,
Dunstable & Watford

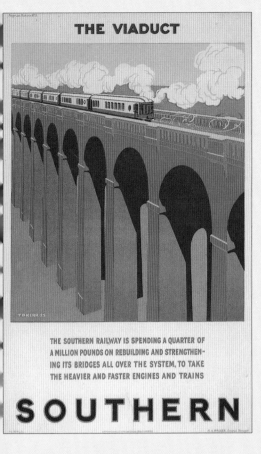

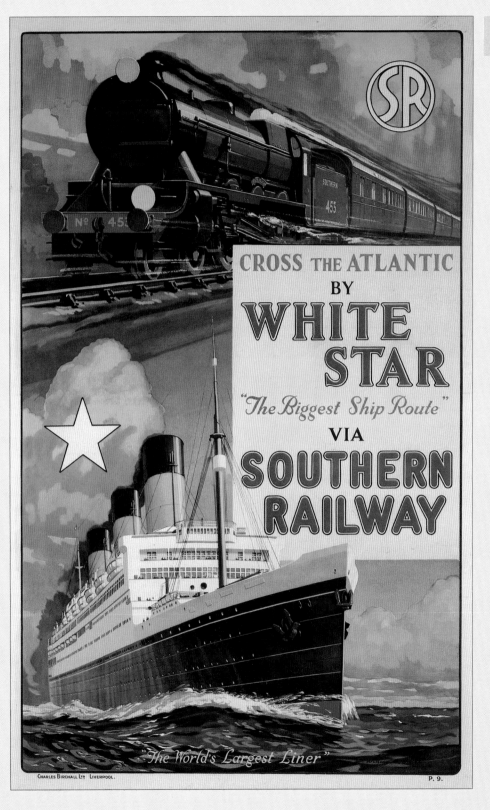

William McDowell
CROSS THE ATLANTIC BY WHITE STAR
c. 1925

Printed by Charles Birchall Ltd, Liverpool

Posters reporting progress served a dual purpose. They informed the general public that the progress of new works was in hand and gave the date when improved facilities would become available. They also satisfied the shareholders that their money was being usefully spent. The Southern did not hesitate to emphasize the progress it was making towards a more modern and exciting railway. The first two posters in this series deal with progress on electrification and the building of new steam locomotives; the third features the famous Ouse Viaduct, on the route between London and Brighton, to highlight bridge-strengthening. The final poster reported on rolling stock. It boasted that 850 new coaches were being built for the Southern's £8 million electrification scheme.

Gregory Brown
THE LONDONER'S GARDEN, KENT
1926

Printed by Adams Bros & Shardlow Ltd, London

"Where'er the rude and moss-grown beech o'er canopies the glade..."

Ethelbert White
KENTISH HILLS & SURREY DALES
1928

Londoners were constantly encouraged to leave their city and enjoy the surrounding countryside. They were tempted by idyllic country scenes, poetry – and half-fare tickets.

Printed by The Baynard Press, London SW9

Kenneth D. Shoesmith
EASTBOURNE
1929

Printed by Waterlow & Sons Ltd, London, Dunstable & Watford

EASTBOURNE

Official Guide from Publicity Manager, (Dept.3) Information Bureau, Eastbourne. Frequent Expresses and Cheap Fares by

SOUTHERN RAILWAY

SOUTHERN RAILWAY ADVERTISING.   Ad./878/ 4500 1930   WATERLOW & SONS LTD·LITH·LONDON·DUNSTABLE & WATFORD

GLORIOUS HOLIDAYS ABROAD—VENICE.
SANTA MARIA DELLA SALUTE.
FOR TRAVEL DETAILS, APPLY SOUTHERN RAILWAY, CONTINENTAL ENQUIRY OFFICE, VICTORIA STATION, LONDON, OR STATIONS AND TOURIST AGENCIES.

The "GOLDEN ARROW" Service and the "MOTORISTS" Service, leaving Dover

LONDON (Victoria)..dep. 11.0 a.m.   PARIS (Nord)..dep. 12.0 noon   DOVER....dep. 11.0 a.m.   CALAIS......dep. 2.15 p.m.
PARIS (Nord)....arr. 5.40 p.m.   LONDON (Victoria)..arr. 7.0 p.m.   CALAIS....arr. 12.45 p.m.   DOVER......arr. 4.0 p.m.

SOUTHERN RAILWAY

Leonard Richmond
GLORIOUS HOLIDAYS ABROAD –
VENICE
1928

This poster shows the church of Santa Maria della Salute, built between 1631 and 1681 in thanksgiving for deliverance from the plague that had afflicted Venice and left over 50,000 dead. Leonard Richmond also illustrated a booklet about continental travel entitled *Come Abroad With Us* and written by E.P. Leigh Bennett. It described a journey that began in a taxi on the way to Waterloo and continued through Normandy, Brittany, Paris, Belgium, Italy and Germany, before finishing back in London.

Printed by The Avenue Press, London

Kenneth D. Shoesmith
THE "GOLDEN ARROW" SERVICE AND THE "MOTORIST'S" SERVICE LEAVING DOVER
1932

The *Golden Arrow* was introduced as a de-luxe train for first-class Pullman passengers and ran between London and Paris. A special steamer, the *SS Canterbury*, was built to ferry passengers across the Channel. By the time that this poster was published, economic conditions, and a lack of Pullman passengers, had led the Southern to add first- and second-class corridor coaches. However, 1932 was a particularly bad year for cross-Channel traffic and this poster failed to have the desired effect. The Motorist's Service was begun in 1931 using the Autocarrier. This was the first car-ferry to be operated by the Southern and could carry 35 vehicles. The crossing took less than two hours but loading and unloading was a lengthy business. This was before the days of drive-on/drive-off ferries, and cranes and slings had to be used.

Printed by McCorquodale & Co. Ltd, London

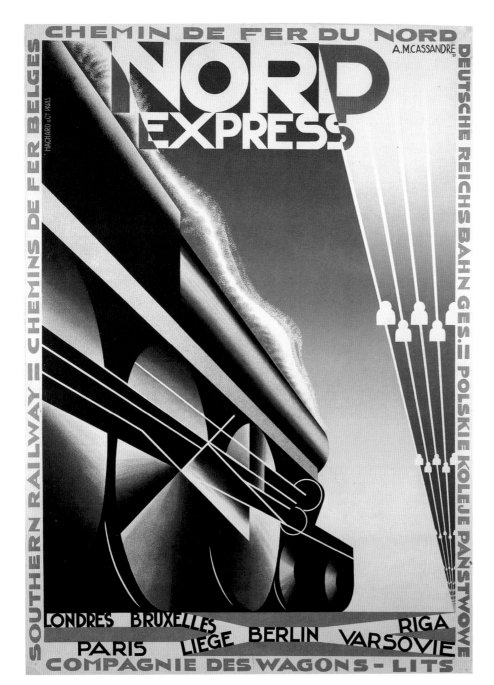

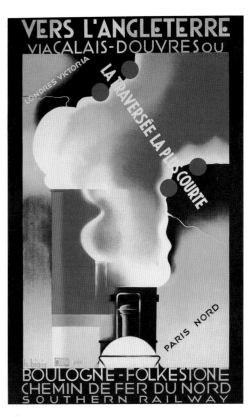

Cassandre
NORD EXPRESS
1927

This was published by the Chemin de Fer du Nord in collaboration with the Southern Railway, Chemins de Fer Belges, Deutsche Reichsbahn, Polskie Koleje Panstwowe and Compagnie des Wagons-Lits. The Nord Express was a de-luxe trans-continental train with wagons lits and Pullman carriages.

Cassandre heralded a new attitude to poster design. He had a great understanding of what the poster should do, and was a poster artist rather than an artist who designed posters. He aimed to communicate, clearly and forcefully, a message about his client's product rather than advance his own personal style. "A painting is an end in itself," he said, "the poster is only a means to an end, a means of communication between the dealer and the public, something like a telegraph."

Until this time trains had rarely appeared in posters: the locomotive was considered to be an aesthetically unappealing machine. Gradually, however, the power, beauty and precision of the locomotive began to be appreciated, and the poster emphasis changed from the places a train served to the train itself. The train became a symbol of movement and power aimed at stimulating an enjoyment of travel for its own sake. The text is included in the design to add to the impact.

Printed by Hachard & Co., Paris

H. Biais
VERS L'ANGLETERRE VIA CALAIS–DOUVRES OU BOULOGNE–FOLKESTONE
c. 1930

A poster issued by the Chemin de Fer du Nord and the Southern Railway for display in France. Both Calais and Boulogne were ports for cargo and passenger services to Dover and Folkestone.

Printed by L. Danel, Lille

70

Edmond Vaughan
SOUTH FOR WINTER SUNSHINE
1929

"One of two artistic winter bills is just to hand from Waterloo," commented the *Railway Gazette* on this poster; "as will be seen, the poster is of curious design, but very effective, the colouring being of a vivid order, and the letterpress consisting of the company's monogram and the words South for Winter Sunshine." The Southern persisted with "impressionist" posters such as this one, even though they often aroused controversy. They were talked about and noticed, even if many disliked them, and so achieved their objective.

Printed by The Baynard Press, London SW9

V. L. Danvers
ENSURE A GOOD MORNING
1933

V. L. Danvers
ENJOY A GOOD NIGHT
1933

These two posters were aimed at commuters, promising them a safe and reliable journey to and from work.

Printed by Ben Johnson & Co. Ltd, London & York

Artist unknown
YOU MAY BE MOVING!
c. 1934

Before the First World War the majority of long-distance furniture removals were carried out by furniture removers and warehousemen who contracted much of the work to the railway companies. The company was a link in the chain and acted as agent for the removers. But, with the rapid development of road transport during the immediate post-war years, business was lost and there was a need to bring it back to the railways. This was done by entering into full competition with the road hauliers. The railway company would handle complete removals from dismantling and packing at one end to unpacking and positioning of furniture in the new home at the other. This poster was part of their publicity campaign. At the same time, the railways, particularly the Southern, were encouraging house-hunters to move out of London to newly developed suburban and rural areas.

Eileen Seyd
FOR YOUR SHOPPING – CHEAP DAY TICKETS
c. 1928

An enticement to off-peak passengers aimed at the female traveller.

Printed by McCorquodale & Co. Ltd, London

J. C. V.
WINTER SUNSHINE
1932

Winter sunshine was strongly promoted by the Southern Railway. Here a city gentleman and his dog leave the grime and smog of London and escape to the south coast.

Printed by The Baynard Press, London SW9

H. Molenaar
SOUTH FOR SUNSHINE
1933

Printed by McCorquodale & Co. Ltd, London

Edmond Vaughan
SO SWIFTLY HOME
1932

The Southern was mainly a passenger railway with a lot of short-distance traffic. With electrification came an acceleration of train services. The system expanded, new houses and stations were built, and more trains ran. Colour-light signalling was the best method of moving trains quickly and safely through a congested area.

Printed by The Baynard Press, London SW9

SOUTHERN RAILWAY

BOURNEMOUTH BELLE

ALL-PULLMAN EXPRESS – SUNDAYS until further notice

	am		pm
WATERLOO	dep.10.30	BOURNEMOUTH C^{TL}	dep.6.20
SOUTHAMPTON WEST	arr.11.59	SOUTHAMPTON WEST	dep.7.0
BOURNEMOUTH C^{TL}	arr.12.39	WATERLOO	arr.8.30

Cheap Return Fares from London to Southampton West 1st 20/-, 3rd 12/6
to Bournemouth C^{TL} 1st 25/-, 3rd 15/- including Pullman Supplement.

It's time to go south

WINTER SPORTS EXPRESSES
leave LONDON (VICTORIA) at
2.0 p.m. Via Calais. 4.20 p.m. Via Boulogne
Full particulars from Continental Enquiry Office
Victoria Station. London. S.W.I. or any Tourist Agency

Audrey Weber
WINTER SPORTS EXPRESSES
1934

Printed by McCorquodale & Co. Ltd, London

H. Molenaar
BOURNEMOUTH BELLE
1933

The *Bournemouth Belle*, an all-Pullman train, was introduced on Saturday 5th July 1931. It left Waterloo daily at 10.30 a.m. and returned at 7.18 p.m. during its first season. It originally had ten Pullman cars but this varied in later years depending on the number of passengers. The *Bournemouth Belle* ran until 9th September 1939 but was then withdrawn and did not reappear until 1946.

Printed by Waterlow & Sons Ltd, London, Dunstable & Watford

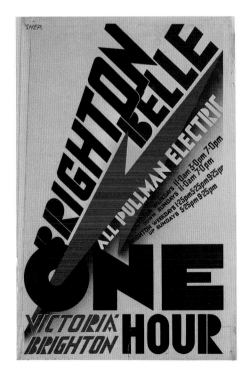

BRIGHTON BELLE
ALL PULLMAN ELECTRIC
ONE HOUR
VICTORIA BRIGHTON

"Shep"
BRIGHTON BELLE
1934

On Friday 29th June 1934 the *Southern Belle* was renamed the *Brighton Belle*. On the same day the world's largest sea-water swimming pool opened at Brighton, and the two events shared the publicity. Three trains ran each way between London (Victoria) and Brighton each day, with two on Sundays. They had both first- and third-class accommodation and followed the usual Pullman practice of charging a supplement for the greater degree of comfort and luxury. The first-class coaches were given names that were fashionable for girls in the 1930s – Hazel, Doris, Audrey, Vera, Gwen and Mona. The *Brighton Belle* became a much-loved train, and there was great sadness when the last service ran on 30th April 1972.

Pat Keely
SOUTHERN FOR THE CONTINENT
1933

The Southern had the advantage of being the major continental holiday conveyors. They advertised "The Peerless Riviera" and offered hints on foreign hotels, passports, trains and reservations.

Printed by McCorquodale & Co. Ltd, London

Cassandre
NEW NIGHT SERVICE
1932

This is the English version of a poster produced jointly by the Southern, Northern Railway of France and ALA Steamship Company. The French version emphasizes Dunkerque, and Victoria was replaced by Folkestone which was the port used on the English side of the Channel. The service was later transferred to Dover with the construction of new train-ferry facilities there. In *Making a Poster* Austin Cooper described the poster in glowing terms: "We are told at once what it is all about – from Victoria via Dunkerque at night. We are also told, forcefully and dramatically, that we shall be guided on our way, our path illuminated by friendly beams of light. First-rate propaganda and beautiful design." He concluded: "if genius is ever to be found linked with commercial art we need look no further."

Printed by L. Danel, Lille

I'M TAKING AN EARLY HOLIDAY 'COS I KNOW SUMMER COMES SOONEST IN THE SOUTH
1936

SI, SONO VENUTO IN INGHILTERRA
1936

These posters were among many reproduced from a snapshot taken in 1924 by commercial photographer Charles E. Brown at the end of one of the platforms at Waterloo Station. The original photograph was reprinted numerous times in several different guises. It showed a small boy with spectacles and suitcase speaking to the driver. The snapshot was sent in to the Publicity Department at Waterloo who arranged for the printers to enlarge it and make a photographic print. It was claimed that the resulting poster had a lifelike quality not previously achieved. Three thousand copies were printed. When the poster was issued the Southern Railway offered to present a framed copy, with a framed photograph of a "King Arthur" class

locomotive, to the boy shown, whose identity was then unknown. Quite a number of parents took their children to the offices at Waterloo but all were sent away disappointed. Eventually the little boy was found to have emigrated to California with his father who was formerly employed in the Electrical Department at Waterloo. The boy was called Ronald Witt.

Other versions of the poster included one issued to advertise the Penny-a-Week Red Cross Fund, as well as French and German language editions. The most recent was produced by British Railways and featured the little boy, complete with teddy bear, standing by an Intercity 125 train.

Printed by Johnson, Riddle & Co. Ltd, London SE1

Audrey Weber
CONDUCTED RAMBLES – SPRING
1936

Audrey Weber
CONDUCTED RAMBLES – SUMMER
1936

Audrey Weber
CONDUCTED RAMBLES – AUTUMN
1935

Farming images are used in these posters to highlight the changes that ramblers see during the seasons. The fourth poster in the series, of winter, depicts a rider in the snow with holly, mistletoe and fir cones.

Printed by Waterlow & Sons Ltd, London & Dunstable

Pat Keely
SOUTHAMPTON CENTRAL STATION
1936

Printed by McCorquodale & Co. Ltd, London

Leslie Carr
SOUTHAMPTON DOCKS
1936

Printed by Waterlow & Sons Ltd, London & Dunstable

The Southern owned Southampton Docks and carried out a major programme of investment during the 1920s and 1930s. The Docks were expanded westwards, where land was available, and facilities greatly improved. Southampton West Station was enlarged to cope with the extra traffic and renamed Southampton Central in 1935. The improvements attracted more shipping. The *Queen Mary* first arrived at Southampton from the Clyde on 27 March 1936.

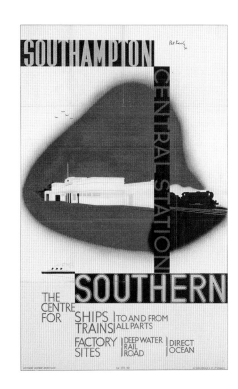

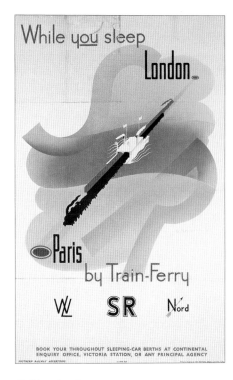

G. Massiot Brown
WHILE *YOU* SLEEP, LONDON–PARIS BY TRAIN–FERRY
1937

"While *you* sleep" suggests that the passenger can enjoy oblivion while those responsible for his or her safety are wide awake. Passengers travelling by train-ferry would get into their sleeping berths at Victoria, completing the journey to Paris without a break. Tickets were checked on arrival.

In the Southern booklet *Travelling South in the Reigns of the Six King Georges*, Helen McKie described how the journey to the continent had improved during the years from 1714 to 1937. She listed the perils facing the eighteenth-century traveller, including the appalling condition of the roads, badly constructed coaches and the risks of meeting highwaymen, not to mention turnpike legislation, the levying of tolls, the length of the journey and the dangers of drunken coachmen and inclement weather.

By comparison, the journey in 1937 was pure joy. It began with "the distinct thrill on arriving at Victoria and seeing the sumptuous blue coaches bearing the lettering 'Compagnie Internationale des Wagons-Lits' and labelled 'London–Paris'. The Wagons-Lits Company have excelled themselves in these new coaches specially built for the train-ferry, with their blue lacquer walls, chromium fittings, mirrors, bells, lights everywhere – even the waterbottle in its neat little cupboard looks like a handsome gin decanter."

Printed by The Baynard Press, London SW9

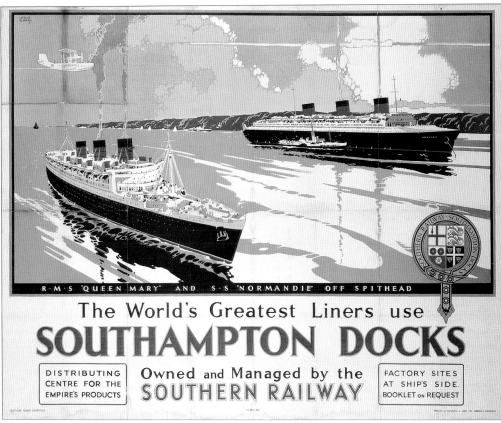

Helen Ray Marshall
TO YOUR LIBRARIES, LECTURES, MUSEUMS
1937

The Southern makes its contribution to the cultural and spiritual welfare of its travellers! Another poster in this series promotes concerts, musical societies and music lessons.

Printed by The Baynard Press, London SW9

Libis
"HINTS FOR HOLIDAYS"
1938

Printed by Waterlow & Sons Ltd, London & Dunstable

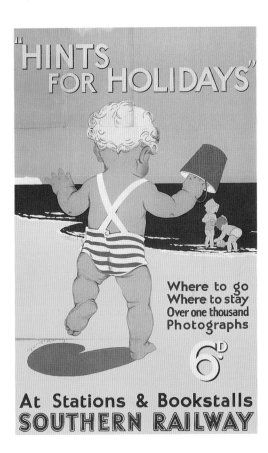

Muriel Harris
"HINTS FOR HOLIDAYS"
1939

(Left) A typically homely Southern Railway poster on a par with Sunny South Sam and the little boy who thinks that "Summer Comes Soonest in the South". It is a sharp contrast to the 1938 poster advertising *Hints for Holidays* (above).

Printed by Waterlow & Sons Ltd, London & Dunstable

H. Alker Tripp
FRESH AIR FOR HEALTH!
1937

The Southern published guides and
promoted them along with cheap
tickets for potential ramblers and
walkers.

Printed by Waterlow & Sons Ltd, London &
Dunstable

Charles Pears
SUMMER SERVICES FOR WINTER
VISITORS TO PORTSMOUTH,
SOUTHSEA & ISLE OF WIGHT
1937

It was the custom of the Southern to issue a striking poster to advertise each of its successive electrification extensions. The route to Portsmouth saw more trains and faster services, in winter as well as summer, after the line was electrified and, as expected, the number of passengers increased.

Printed by Waterlow & Sons Ltd, London & Dunstable

Walter E. Spradbery
THE SOUTH DOWNS
1946

The hills of the south were widely promoted for rambling excursions. According to S. P. B. Mais who wrote a series of guides for the Southern, they offered "that fresh draught of air, natural beauty, complete quietude and communion with the sky and earth . . . that is to be got only on a hill." Another booklet entitled *The South Downs*, written by "The Tramp", began with extracts from the work of Rudyard Kipling, Robert Bridges and Gilbert White. The author went on to explain the geological composition and evolution of the Downs, recommended further instructive reading with a list of places to visit and finished by saying "this is a country worth fighting for." It is to be hoped he was well paid!

Printed by Waterlow & Sons Ltd, London & Dunstable

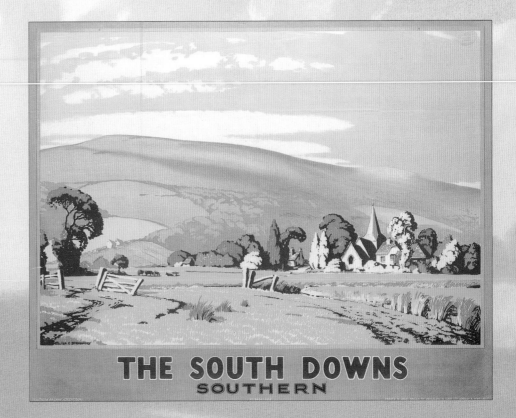

86

Charles Pears
"SUNSET OVER GUERNSEY"
1939

Printed by Waterlow & Sons Ltd, London & Dunstable

Anna Zinkeisen
THE WHITE CLIFFS OF DOVER
1938

Dover has always been one of the most important ports in England and its cliffs have come to symbolize the strength and security of the country. The Southern operated passenger and freight vessels from Dover and introduced both car-ferry and train-ferry services during the 1930s. Anna Zinkeisen produced another poster in this style, again designed to look like a framed painting, showing the "Laying of the Foundation Stone at Southampton Docks".

Printed by The Baynard Press, London SW9

William Brealey
WHY DO THEY CALL ME SUNNY
SOUTH SAM?
1939

Sunny South Sam made his debut in
1930 and quickly became a popular
figure. He was seen in a variety of
guises, including an appearance with a
group of marionettes, and he often
displayed Meteorological Office
sunshine records for the south-coast
resorts.

Printed by Waterlow & Sons Ltd, London &
Dunstable

**Kenneth D. Shoesmith and V. L.
Danvers**
RAMSGATE
1939

Ramsgate "on the Sunshine Coast"
was famous for its boating and
yachting. It was the first and most
convenient harbour for boats
proceeding down the Channel from
either the Thames or the east-coast
ports. Ramsgate Week, the regatta,
attracted a large gathering of racing
yachts and onlookers who were
potential railway customers.

Printed by McCorquodale & Co. Ltd, London

V. L. Danvers
FOLKESTONE
1947

Printed by McCorquodale
& Co. Ltd, London

Norman Wilkinson
THE NEW TS "FALAISE"
1947

The *Falaise* re-opened the passenger service from Southampton to St Malo after the Second World War. It carried 1,527 passengers, up to 31 cars and was equipped with radar and radio telephone facilities. The ship was oil-fired and had a maximum speed of 20 knots per hour.

Printed by The Baynard Press, London

THE RIVER CAMEL NEAR PADSTOW

SEE THE WEST COUNTRY FROM THE TRAIN
BY
SOUTHERN RAILWAY

Eric Hesketh Hubbard
SEE THE WEST COUNTRY FROM THE
TRAIN
1947

Padstow was the furthest point in
Cornwall that could be reached by the
Southern.

Printed by The Baynard Press, London

Severin
THE DEVON BELLE
1947

Printed by The Baynard Press, London

Helen McKie
WATERLOO STATION – WAR
1947

Helen McKie
WATERLOO STATION – PEACE
1947

These two posters were commissioned from Helen McKie as part of the celebrations that took place in 1948 to mark the centenary of the opening of Waterloo Station. Helen McKie carried out a wide range of work for the Southern. In addition to both writing and illustrating booklets and other publicity material, she designed uniforms and upholstery and in 1939 was asked to decorate two new coaches for the cross-Channel service.

Printed by The Baynard Press, London

Artist unknown
SWEET ROTHESAY BAY
1923

One of the first Clyde resorts, Rothesay, was blessed with a busy pier, beautiful gardens and an elegant bandstand. It also boasted commodious hotels, boarding houses, hydros, villas and apartments ranging from the de luxe to the homely, and laid claim to restorative air, pinewoods, electric trams and red fuchsia that flowered all the year round. It was served by LMS steamers.

Printed by Dobson Molle & Co. Ltd, Edinburgh & London

E.W. Haslehust
ALTON TOWERS AND GARDENS
c. 1923

Printed by Thos Forman & Sons Ltd, Nottingham

Warwick Goble
STRATFORD-UPON-AVON
c. 1923

As the birthplace of William Shakespeare, Stratford-upon-Avon was promoted extensively to the American market.

Printed by Greycaine Ltd, London & Watford

The five posters on these pages formed part of the series of sixteen commissioned by the LMS from members of the Royal Academy in 1924. Each artist was paid a fee of £100 and received royalties on the sale of prints.

Sir William Orpen
THE NIGHT MAIL – THE ENGINEMEN
1924

Printed by Bemrose & Sons Ltd

Stanhope Forbes
THE PERMANENT WAY – RELAYING
1924

Two posters portrayed the railway: "The Night Mail" and "The Permanent Way". The idea of, as the *Railway Gazette* put it in 1910, "using the railway to advertise the railway", had developed before the First World War when several companies had featured locomotives on their posters and publicity material. The use of other railway subjects was not widespread, although one notable exception was the poster "The Best Permanent Way in the World" by Norman Wilkinson. This was issued by the London and North Western Railway in 1910 to draw attention to the good riding quality of its track.

Printed by Jordison & Co. Ltd, London

Arnesby Brown
NOTTINGHAM CASTLE – THE CENTRE OF MEDIAEVAL ENGLAND
1924

No fewer than five posters showing castles were produced for the scheme but this was the most impressive. Brown's view lacked the picturesque qualities of the other four, showing the castle as it appeared across factory rooftops and smoking chimneys.

Printed by Thos Forman & Sons, Nottingham

Charles Sims
LONDON
1924

Printed by McCorquodale & Co. Ltd

LMS NOTTINGHAM CASTLE.
THE CENTRE OF MEDIÆVAL ENGLAND.
BY ARNESBY BROWN. R.A.

Sir Bertram MacKennal
SPEED
1924

This poster became a constant source of fascination on station platforms. It was made from a clay relief model which was photographed to produce the poster, and the final image gave a strong impression of three-dimensionality. Norman Wilkinson said at the time, "I have seen a porter go and try it with his nail to see if it really was flat." The figure in the poster represents Icarus, the first man to fly. This seems a rather strange choice of subject since, according to legend, Icarus flew too near to the sun, melted the wax of his wings and fell into the sea. No matter how fast the locomotive, no passenger would have boarded the train if it was not going to reach its destination!

Printed by Waterlow & Sons Ltd, London, Dunstable & Watford

LMS LONDON
BY CHARLES SIMS. R.A.

LMS SPEED
BY SIR BERTRAM MACKENNAL. R.A.

LMS

Ralph & Brown
FIND RADIANT HEALTH AT
LLANDRINDOD-WELLS
c. 1923

Published jointly by the LMS, Great
Western and Town Association of
Llandrindod Wells.

Printed by Jordison & Co. Ltd, London &
Middlesbrough

Norman Howard
SCOTLAND – STRAIGHT AS THE CROW
FLIES
c. 1924

LMS The Best Way series no. 21. "The
Best Way" was a slogan carried over
from the Midland Railway and used
extensively by the LMS.

Printed by McCorquodale & Co. Ltd, London

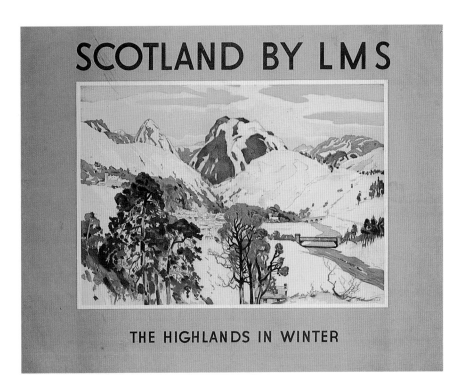

SCOTLAND BY LMS

THE HIGHLANDS IN WINTER

George Nicholls
THE HIGHLANDS IN WINTER
c. 1924

The LMS ran to Inverness and beyond, along the old Highland Railway route.

Printed by Jarrold & Sons Ltd, Norwich & London

S.J. Lamorna Birch
BUXTON
1924

Printed by Thos Forman & Sons, Nottingham

LMS BUXTON
THE MOUNTAIN SPA
BY S.J. LAMORNA BIRCH. R.W.S.

Montague B. Black
SPEND YOUR HOLIDAYS IN THE LAKE
DISTRICT
c. 1924

The LMS promoted the English lakes to
both home and overseas visitors.
Booklets aimed at travellers from the
USA and Canada dwelt particularly on
its literary associations: "Here you are
on the edge of a country – a famous
and beautiful country – which has
given a school of poetry to England
and to which crowds of visitors come
every year, where Wordsworth lived
and died and where all at one time
Southey, Coleridge, De Quincey,
Arnold of Rugby, his son Matthew
Arnold, and Miss Martineau lived and
worked, drawing their inspiration
from the quiet beauty of the
mountains and buildings that England
has not let die."

Printed by McCorquodale & Co. Ltd

F. Whatley
INGLETON – THE LAND OF
WATERFALLS
c. 1924

Printed by McCorquodale & Co. Ltd

Artist unknown
A TOTAL ECLIPSE OF THE SUN
1927

One of the most unusual events of the inter-war years was the total eclipse of the sun which took place on 29 June 1927. This was the first total eclipse since 1724, and it lasted for only 24 seconds. It created an enormous amount of excitement, and the LMS, LNER and Great Western all ran special trains for the occasion. The "totality band" stretched from North Wales across to Hartlepool and Middlesbrough. The LMS claimed that the best place to view the eclipse was Southport as it was right in the centre of the band, and produced three posters to advertise the event, together with leaflets and other publicity material. It carried over 70,000 people on its special trains which included a series of restaurant-car expresses from Euston.

Printed by McCorquodale, Glasgow & London

P. Irwin Brown
LIVERPOOL & MANCHESTER RAILWAY
CENTENARY CELEBRATIONS
1930

The railway companies were not slow to advertise special events of their own. The centenary celebrations of the Liverpool and Manchester Railway in 1930 were heavily promoted. The celebrations were held at Liverpool between 13th and 20th September 1930. Engines including the *Novelty* and the *Planet* were on view alongside the very latest locomotives. There were miniature railway systems and a pageant of transport every evening at 7 p.m. Some of the more picturesque scenes featured Egyptian transport in Cleopatra's reign, Spanish transport in Don Quixote's days, a Red Indian attack on a covered wagon convoy, a stagecoach hold-up by highwaymen, Liverpool life in 1830 (showing stagecoach arrivals, sedan chairs and hobby horses), Lancashire witches in session and an attack on the surveyors of the Liverpool and Manchester line! At the end of each evening there was a firework display.

Alfred Lambart
SPEND A DAY AT PORT SUNLIGHT
c. 1926

For a day out with a difference the LMS suggested a visit to the soap factory of Lever Brothers at Port Sunlight and the adjacent garden village. Parties were conducted around the factory by guides and shown the soap boiling, packing, box-making and printing departments before taking tea at Hulme Hall or the Lady Lever Art Gallery.

Spend a day at
PORT SUNLIGHT
GARDEN VILLAGE & MODEL WORKS
CHEAP RETURN TICKETS FOR PARTIES OF EIGHT OR MORE
PARTICULARS AT THE BOOKING OFFICE

TRAVEL LMS   TRAVEL LMS

Norman Wilkinson
GOLF IN NORTHERN IRELAND – THE 8TH GREEN AT PORTRUSH
c. 1925

Norman Wilkinson was commissioned to produce a series of posters illustrating the many different sports and pastimes that could be enjoyed within the area covered by the LMS. "In the territory of the LMS system," he said, "one finds every possible form of sport – salmon and trout fishing, shooting, hunting, yachting, racing, deer stalking and, of course, the best of golf. Few people realise also that in Scotland there is plenty of good skiing, or know that many experienced climbers prefer the mountains of Wales and the English Lake District to the snowfields of the Alps."

Printed by S.C. Allen & Co. Ltd, 4 Lisle St., London WC2

Paul Henry
CONNEMARA
1926

The LMS made many of its posters available for sale to the general public: 12,000 were bought between 1924 and 1928. This was the most popular, selling over 1,500 copies.

Printed by S.C. Allen & Co. Ltd, 4 Lisle St., London WC2

Artist unknown
PERRY BARR, BIRMINGHAM – "THE GOODWOOD OF GREYHOUND RACING"
1928

Greyhound racing was introduced into Britain from the USA in the 1920s and the first races were run at Belle Vue in Manchester. This poster was produced for the opening of the stadium at Perry Bar and shows the new sport trying to project an attractive and stylish image.

Printed by James Cond Ltd, Offset Printers, Birmingham

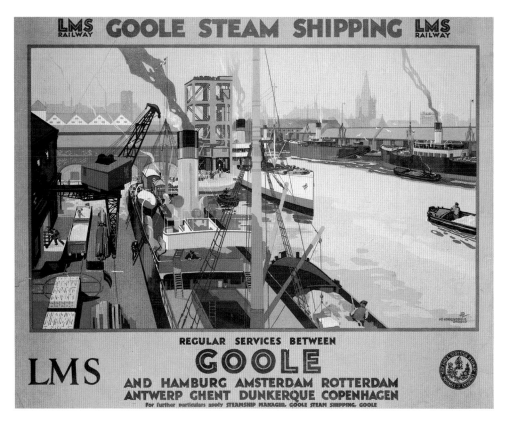

J. P./McCorquodale Studio
REGULAR SERVICES BETWEEN GOOLE
AND HAMBURG, AMSTERDAM,
ROTTERDAM, ANTWERP, GHENT,
DUNKERQUE, COPENHAGEN
c. 1928

Printed by McCorquodale, Glasgow & London

Norman Wilkinson
PUT YOUR PLANT WHERE IT WILL
GROW
c. 1928

The LMS promoted trade custom as
well as tourism. Factories, railhead
distribution and exceptional loads
were encouraged. For machinery and
engineering products that were too
bulky or too heavy to be carried in
ordinary goods wagons and vans, the
company built special wagons.
Nothing was too big for the LMS!

Printed by McCorquodale & Co. Ltd

LMS

Reginald Higgins
ISLE OF MAN – THE LANDING OF KING ORRY
c. 1929

King Orry was Godred Crovan, the first known King of the Isle of Man. He fought with the Norwegians under Harald, King of Norway, against Harold of England at Stamford Bridge in 1066 and fled to Man following the English victory. In 1079 he gathered together an army and fleet and took over the island. He is remembered for uniting the Isles of Man into one kingdom. Crovan was a nickname meaning "white gauntlets" which he supposedly always wore. The Manx form of Godred was Goree and the words King Goree became King Oree or Orry.

Printed by Charles & Read Ltd, London

Artist unknown
SPEND YOUR SUMMER HOLIDAYS AT
BLACKPOOL IN JUNE
c. 1925

Printed by Gazette & Herald, Colour Printers,
Blackpool

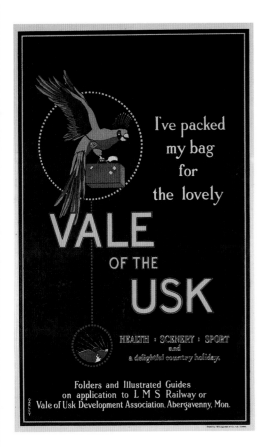

Alfred Oakley
VALE OF THE USK
c. 1930

Printed by McCorquodale & Co. Ltd, London

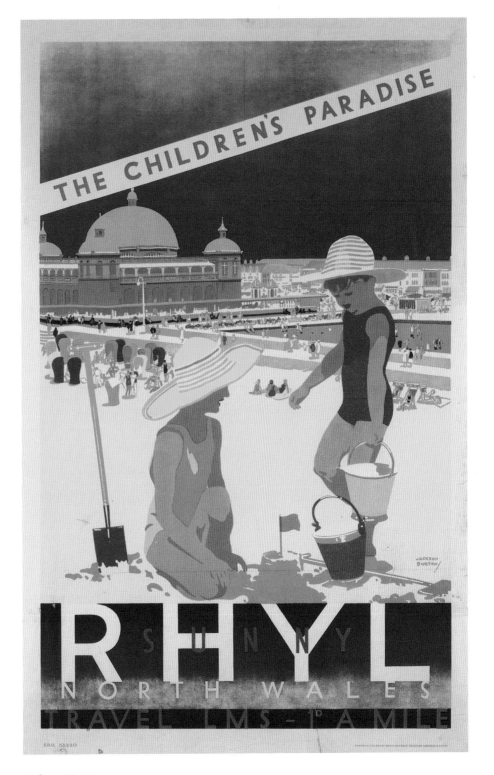

Jackson Burton
SUNNY RHYL — THE CHILDREN'S
PARADISE
c. 1930

Printed by Beck & Inchbold Ltd, Leeds, London &
Glasgow

SEA, SUNSHINE AND SPORT
LYTHAM ST. ANNES
ILLUSTRATED GUIDE ON APPLICATION TO TOWN CLERK, LYTHAM ST. ANNES

Charles Pears
LYTHAM ST. ANNES
c. 1930

Printed by Charles & Read Ltd, London

LMS

Septimus E. Scott
NEW BRIGHTON & WALLASEY
c. 1930

GUIDE BOOK ON APPLICATION TO TOWN CLERK WALLASEY

NEW BRIGHTON
& WALLASEY
SERVED BY LMS

FOR PARTICULARS OF CHEAP FARES & TRAIN SERVICES APPLY ANY LMS STATION OR AGENCY

Spencer Pryse
THE FAMOUS BATHING POOL AT
HASTINGS & ST LEONARDS
c. 1933

Printed by McCorquodale & Co. Ltd, London

LMS "ROYAL SCOT" LEAVES EUSTON
BY
NORMAN WILKINSON, R.I.

Norman Wilkinson
"ROYAL SCOT" LEAVES EUSTON
c. 1930

The *Royal Scot* ran between Euston and Glasgow. The LMS issued route books with the title *The Track of the Royal Scot* which described the scenery and highlights of the journey.

Printed by McCorquodale & Co. Ltd, Glasgow & London

Artist unknown
NORTH STAFFORD HOTEL, STOKE-ON-TRENT
c. 1933

The LMS was the largest owner of railway hotels in the world, controlling over 30 establishments.

Printed by James Cond Ltd, London & Birmingham

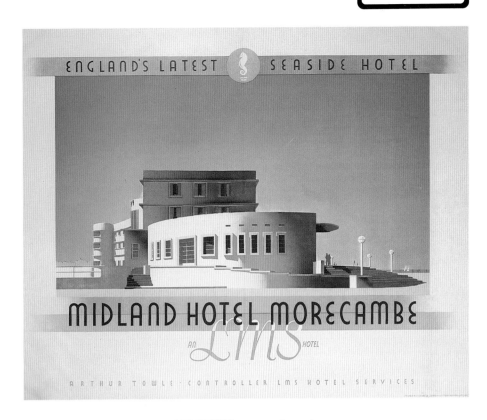

Artist unknown
MIDLAND HOTEL, MORECAMBE
1933

Designed by Oliver Hill, the Midland Hotel was one of the first modernist public buildings. Arthur Towle, the LMS Hotel Services Controller, was alarmed by the proposed design and thought it would frighten off traditional visitors. The main spiral staircase was an innovation, and Eric Ravilious was commissioned to paint a mural in the café. Unfortunately, this faded badly soon after the hotel opened, due to soaked walls and peeling paint, but has now been lovingly restored by the present management. What was once a hotel for the young sophisticated set is now largely visited by the retired, possibly the same guests who stayed there in the 1930s. The seahorse became the emblem of the Midland Hotel after it was rebuilt in 1933. Two were carved in stone by the sculptor Eric Gill and placed above the entrance. Oliver Hill also remodelled the interior of the Euston Hotel in London and designed an American bar at St Pancras, as well as a first-class dining saloon.

Printed by Jordison & Co. Ltd, London & Middlesbrough

LMS

Norman Wilkinson
BRITANNIA TUBULAR BRIDGE, MENAI
STRAITS
c. 1934

The Britannia Tubular Bridge opened
in 1850. Designed by Robert
Stephenson, it linked the Welsh
mainland with Anglesey and the port
of Holyhead. In 1970 it was badly
damaged by fire and was
reconstructed using steel arched spans
in place of the original tubes. It was
further altered in 1980 when a road
was added above the rail deck.

Printed by Jordison & Co. Ltd, London &
Middlesbrough

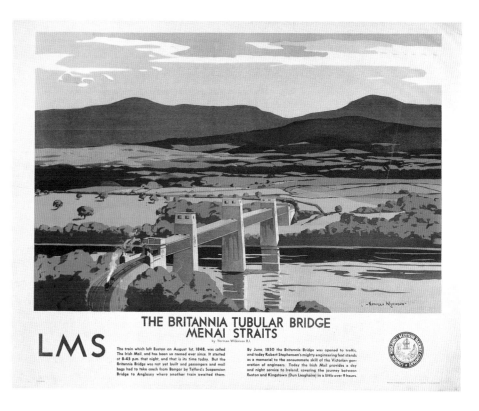

C. Baker
SNOWDONIA
c. 1933

In 1923 the LMS boasted in its booklet
The Wonderland of Wales that
"Snowdon and the Welsh Highlands
are synonymous with scenery of
ravishing beauty. Ancient story, sweet
murmurs of mountain streams and
soul stirring music of peasant people
add to the delights of this romantic
region as a holiday ground." The
booklet also contained information on
the Snowdon Mountain Railway and
the Festiniog Railway. It was at pains
to assure the potential passenger that
such railways were completely safe,
despite their steep gradients, and that
"any perturbations he may feel will
vanish after he has experienced a few
minutes in the train."

Printed by Jordison & Co. Ltd, London &
Middlesbrough

Charles Pears
SOUTHEND-ON-SEA – NIGHT SCENE
OFF PIERHEAD
c. 1933

A romantic view of Southend-on-Sea
issued jointly by the LMS and LNER.

Printed by Jordison, London

NIGHT SCENE OFF PIERHEAD
BY CHAS. PEARS R.O.I.

LMS SOUTHEND-ON-SEA L·N·E·R

ILLUSTRATED GUIDE FROM LMS OR L·N·E·R STATION OR ENQUIRY OFFICE OR FROM THE CORPORATION ENQUIRY BUREAU, SOUTHEND-ON-SEA

Norman Wilkinson
TILBURY FOR THE CONTINENT
c. 1934

The *SS Picard* featured in this poster became a railway ship in 1929. It had a gross tonnage of 2,255. This is very typical of Norman Wilkinson's style: the sea and sky reflect each other to give depth to the whole image.

Printed by S.C. Allen & Co. Ltd, 4 Lisle St., London WC2

Norman Wilkinson
LAUNCH OF *TSS DUKE OF YORK*.
QUEEN'S ISLAND, BELFAST
1935

Built in 1935 by Harland and Wolff of Belfast, the *Duke of York* operated on the Heysham to Belfast service. It became a troop transport vessel during the Second World War and was involved in the Dieppe raid of August 1942.

Printed by London Lithographic Co., SE5

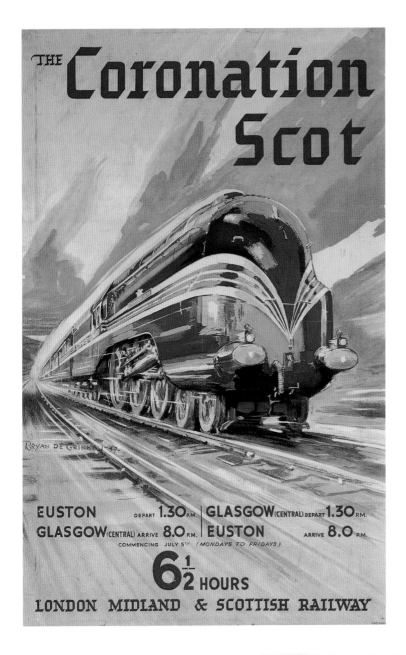

The *Coronation Scot* was the first streamlined Anglo-Scottish express to travel between Euston and Glasgow Central. Trains left both stations simultaneously at 1.30 p.m. and reached their destinations at 8 p.m. The streamlined locomotives had four silver-painted bands starting from a V-point at the front and running at window height along the length of the train. Five locomotives operated the service: *Coronation*, *Queen Elizabeth*, *Queen Mary*, *Princess Alice* and *Princess Alexandra*. These were designed by William Stanier and built by the LMS at Crewe Works. The locomotive *Coronation* reached a speed of 114 m.p.h. on a demonstration run from Euston to Crewe in 1937.

Bryan de Grineau
THE CORONATION SCOT
1937

Lili Réthi
CREWE WORKS – BUILDING
"CORONATION" CLASS ENGINES
1937

Printed by Jordison, London

LMS

Frank Ball
GRANGE OVER SANDS
c. 1935

Printed by Beck & Inchbold Ltd, London, Leeds & Glasgow

Arthur Watts
A MAP OF THE LAKE DISTRICT
1935

A series of amusing views – including the unlikely sight of the Loch Ness Monster asking for directions to Windermere – makes this a poster with a sense of humour. The wonderful network of lakes and mountains is clearly indicated on the map and there are thumbnail sketches of local and social interest, such as William Wordsworth's cottage and the Roman Villa at Ravenglass. Sadly Arthur Watts died in the same year.

Printed by Group of Associated Printers

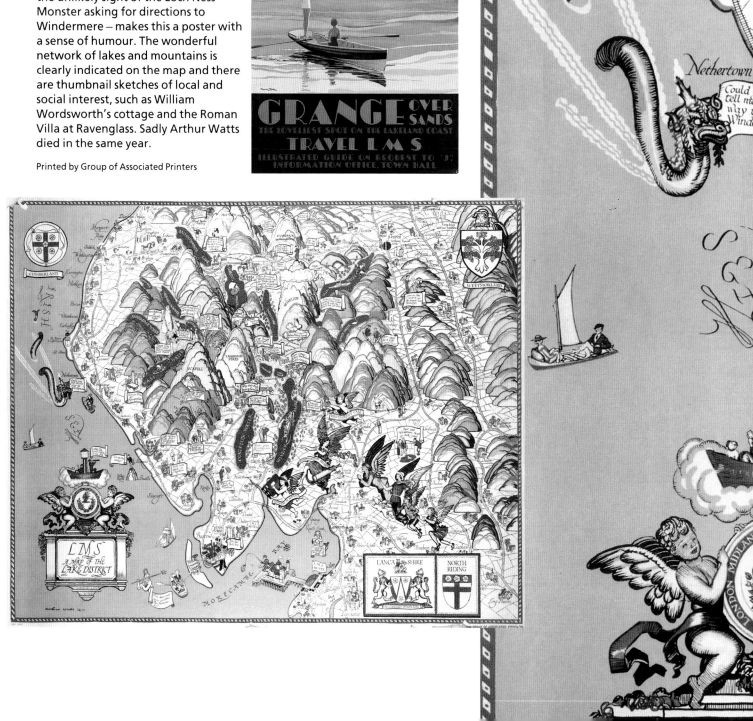

LMS

120

Bruce Angrave
COME TO CROMER
c. 1937

Produced jointly by the LMS and LNER.
This area in Norfolk was commonly
known as "Poppyland".

Printed by John Horn Ltd, London & Glasgow

Light
CRYSTAL PALACE ROAD CIRCUIT —
GRAND COMPOSITE MEETING
1938

The Crystal Palace motor-racing circuit
opened in 1937 and closed in 1972. The
Sydenham Trophy was run over fifteen
laps of the two-mile circuit, and cars
were grouped and handicapped
according to class. The race in this
particular year was won by John H.T.
Smith in an MG with an average speed
of 52.77 m.p.h. LMS passengers could
book direct to Crystal Palace which was
served by the Southern. The Crystal
Palace itself had been destroyed by fire
in 1936. Two water towers did survive
(one of which is shown in the poster)
but were demolished in 1940 as they
were thought to be used as
navigational aids by German aircraft
on their way to bomb London.

Printed by Haycock Press, London

Christopher Clark
LONDON – ST. JAMES'S PALACE
c. 1937

One of many posters by Christopher Clark depicting the pageantry of Britain, and particularly London. Others include "The Opening of Parliament", "The Horse Guards" and "Trooping of the Colour", as well as "The Highland Games" and "Stirling Castle".

Printed by McCorquodale & Co. Ltd, Glasgow & London

LONDON: St. James's Palace
By Christopher Clark, R.I.

LMS

In 1530, King Henry VIII, tiring of Kennington, built himself a "goodly manor" at St. James's as a country seat. Formerly there had been a religious house there, founded "before the time of man's memory." To-day, St. James's Palace is the official residence of H.R.H. the Prince of Wales, and here, according to ancient practice, the Changing of the King's Guard of His Majesty's Foot Guards, accompanied by one of their magnificent bands, is made at 10.45 a.m. (on Sundays at 9.45 a.m.); though during recent years, when His Majesty is in London, the actual ceremony of Changing the Guard is in the Courtyard of Buckingham Palace and a detachment of the King's Guard is mounted at St. James's Palace.

LMS

122

Norman Wilkinson
HARROW SCHOOL
1937

Printed by S.C. Allen & Co. Ltd, London W1

Norman Wilkinson
REPTON SCHOOL
1937

Printed by McCorquodale, Glasgow

These two posters form part of a series entitled "Famous Public Schools on the LMS". Each contains information on the history and customs of the school depicted, and bears the crest of both the school and the LMS. Others in the series include Bedford, Berkhamsted, Fettes, Mill Hill, Oundle, Rugby, St Paul's (London), Sedbergh, Shrewsbury, Stonyhurst, Stowe, Uppingham and Westminster.

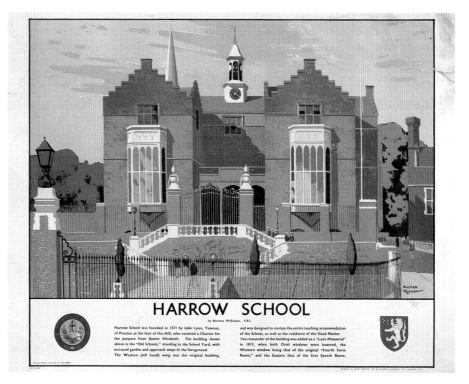

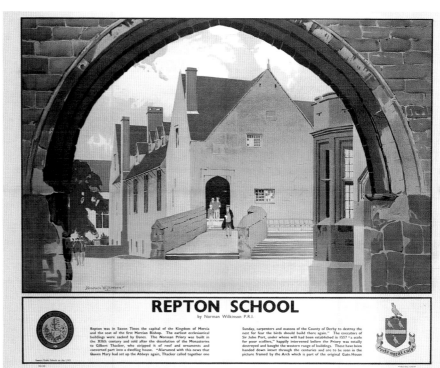

LMS   THE DAY BEGINS

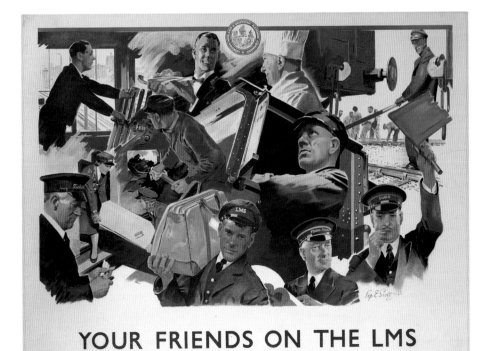

YOUR FRIENDS ON THE LMS

Terence Cuneo
THE DAY BEGINS
1946

An early railway poster by Terence
Cuneo who had produced his first
design, of an Essex watermill, for the
LNER in 1942. He later worked for
British Railways and is still active today.

Printed by Jordison & Co. Ltd, London

Septimus E. Scott
YOUR FRIENDS ON THE LMS
1946

In this poster the LMS draws attention
to the varied public service provided by
its employees. Some of the portraits
were based on actual photographs of
LMS staff.

Printed by Jordison & Co. Ltd, London

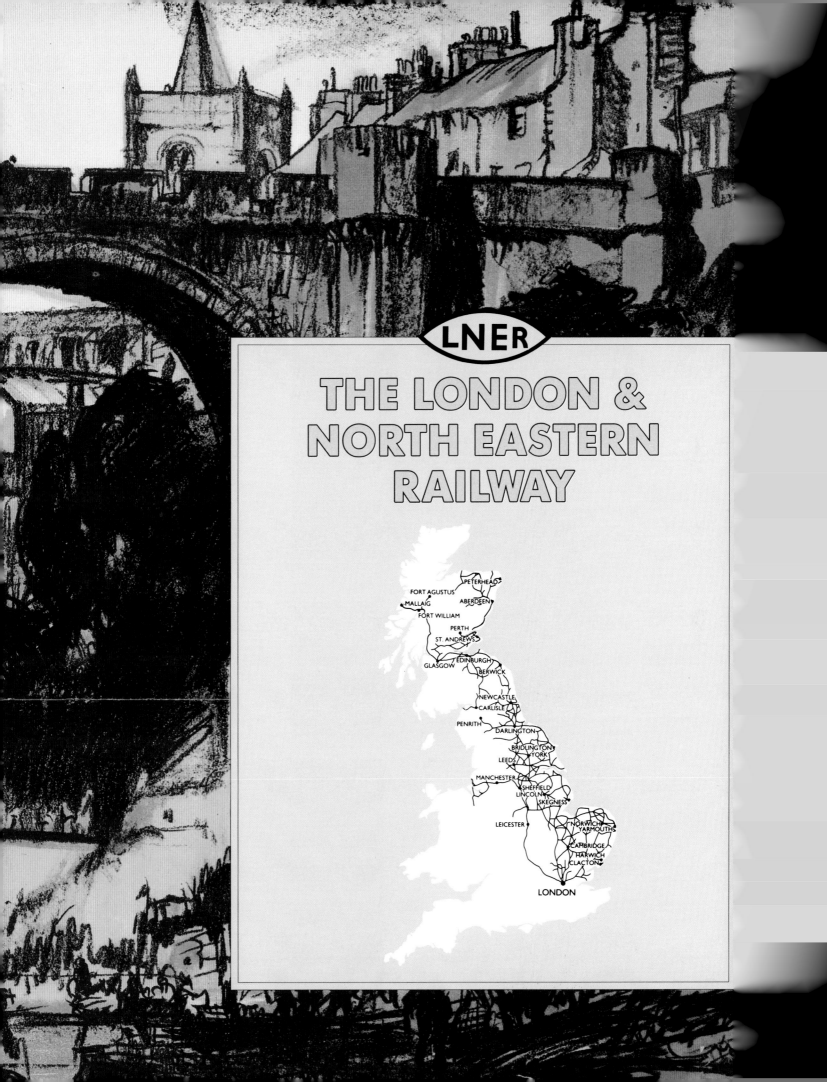

LNER

THE LONDON & NORTH EASTERN RAILWAY

PETERHEAD

FORT AGUSTUS

MALLAIG
FORT WILLIAM
ABERDEEN

PERTH

ST. ANDREWS

EDINBURGH

GLASGOW
BERWICK

NEWCASTLE
CARLISLE

PENRITH
DARLINGTON

BRIDLINGTON
YORK

LEEDS

MANCHESTER
SHEFFIELD
LINCOLN

SKEGNESS

LEICESTER
NORWICH
YARMOUTHS

CAMBRIDGE
HARWICH
CLACTON

LONDON

Frank Brangwyn
OVER THE NIDD NEAR HARROGATE
1924

The first Royal Academician to work for a railway company was Frank Brangwyn who produced a series of posters for the LNER. These included views of the Royal Border Bridge at Berwick-upon-Tweed, the Forth Bridge and the High Level Bridge at Newcastle upon Tyne, as well as this one of Knaresborough Viaduct. Brangwyn was unusual in that he was one of the few poster artists who lithographed his own work rather than leaving it to printers.

Printed by the Avenue Press, London WC2

Fred Taylor
YORK MINSTER – ENGLAND'S TREASURE HOUSE OF STAINED GLASS
1923

This was the first LNER poster issued. Fred Taylor had previously worked for the Midland Railway and London Transport. He went on to become the LNER's most prolific artist. The poster shows the "Five Sisters" window in the North Transept of York Minster. Issued with it was an illustrated brochure. Copies of the poster were for sale at ten shillings and sixpence. The original painting was put on display at the Royal Institute of British Architects in London. Both painting and poster met with immediate acclaim. "The artist, Mr Fred Taylor, has most happily caught, and the printer has no less finely reproduced, the dim, religious light of York's magnificent fane," commented the *Railway Gazette*, "and both may be warmly congratulated on the excellence of their work."

Printed by John Waddington Ltd, Leeds & London

Fred Taylor
LONDON
1925

Printed by Eyre & Spottiswoode Ltd, London

THE BROADS

200 MILES SAFE INLAND WATERWAYS

HOLIDAYS AFLOAT £4 PER WEEK

PARTICULARS OF TRAIN SERVICE, FARES ETC. FROM L·N·E·R INQUIRY OFFICES OR STATIONS. DESCRIPTIVE GUIDE (PRICE 6ᵈ) FROM NORFOLK BROADS BUREAU, BROADLAND HOUSE, NEWGATE STREET, LONDON, E.C.I.

Spencer Pryse
THE BROADS
c. 1925

An LNER booklet claimed that there was nowhere else in England where a jaded businessman could so easily find "a restful remoteness from the wearying stress of city life" than the Broads, and compared them to the Adirondack Lakes in New York State. The booklet was one of twenty published in the *Holidays* series. The others made similarly outstanding claims.

Printed by Vincent Brooks, Day & Son Ltd, London WC2

W. H. Barribal
BRIDLINGTON
c. 1925

It would seem, from this poster, that all bathing beauties in Bridlington were identical and that the menfolk, in general, stayed at home!

Printed by John Waddington Ltd, Leeds & London

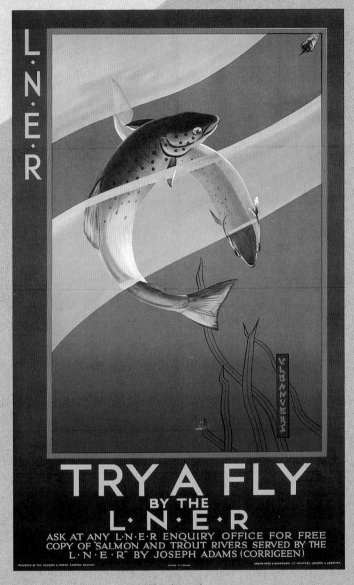

V. L. Danvers
TRY A FLY
1925

One of a set of three posters. The other two were of a duck and a grouse designed to attract the gunman to the Norfolk Broads and Scotland respectively. This one was aimed at persuading the fly fisherman to ply his sport in Scotland and the North of England.

Printed by Adams Bros & Shardlow Ltd, London & Leicester

Alfred Lambart
TYNEMOUTH
1926

This poster came out just before the General Strike. In economic terms 1926 was a bad year for the railways, especially the LNER. The company had lost much of its freight income and its revenue was depleted. It was afterwards said that the only bright feature for the railways during 1926 was the publicity that had been issued before the Strike in anticipation of record seasonal traffic.

Printed by Ben Johnson & Co. Ltd, York

H.G. Gawthorn
GREAT YARMOUTH & GORLESTON ON SEA
c. 1926

The LNER published booklets entitled *From the Carriage Window* which were intended to provide interest for passengers on train journeys. Volumes in the series included the routes of the *East Anglian*, *The Broadsman*, *The Norfolkman* and *The Easterling*, all of which featured Great Yarmouth and Gorleston. On the back of each booklet was a train speed table indicating time per mile and per quarter mile. At this time Yarmouth boasted a six-mile-long promenade.

Printed by David Allen & Sons Ltd, London

Frank Mason
REMEMBER EAST ANGLIA NEXT SUMMER
1926

An early poster by Frank Mason for the LNER, this was one of a set of six featuring lighthouses around the coast of England and Scotland. Mason had previously worked for the North Eastern Railway and was recognized as an outstanding designer by William Teasdale and Cecil Dandridge. He originally trained as a mariner and engineer before entering the commercial art world, and this background provided the inspiration for his work. Many art galleries have examples of his marine paintings.

Printed by Vincent Brooks, Day & Son Ltd, London WC2

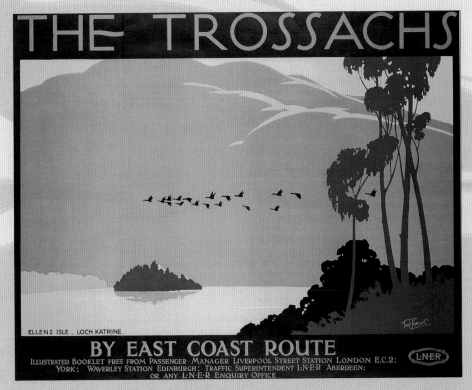

Tom Purvis
THE TROSSACHS – ELLEN'S ISLE, LOCH
KATRINE
c. 1926

Tom Purvis brought respectability to commercial art. "I loathe the word 'artist,'" he said, "personally I am proud of being called a Master Craftsman." In 1930 he was one of a group who banded together to form the Society of Industrial Artists. This tried to put pressure on industry to improve standards of training for commercial artists and widen their scope of employment. Purvis became one of the first Royal Designers for Industry in 1936.

Printed by Haycock, Cadle & Graham Ltd, 80 Fleet Street, EC4 & Camberwell

R.E. Higgins
BELGIUM, HARWICH–ZEEBRUGGE
1927

A 1920s view of continental café society.

Printed by Hancock, Corfield & Waller Ltd, Mitcham, London

A.van Anrooy
OLYMPIC GAMES, AMSTERDAM
1928

Printed by Vincent Brooks, Day & Son Ltd, London WC2

Ludwig Hohlwein
MUNICH AND CENTRAL EUROPE
1929

Ludwig Hohlwein first studied as an
architect, and this is reflected in his
superb sense of layout and visual
balance. He designed travel and
commercial posters as well as political
posters, including work for the Nazis
during the Second World War. He died
at Berchtesgaden in 1949.

Printed by David Allen & Sons Ltd, London

Tom Purvis
MABLETHORPE & SUTTON-ON-SEA
c. 1927

This poster aroused some controversy when it was first issued. The company received an angry letter from the secretary of a society for the prevention of cruelty to animals, protesting that a picture of a child hanging on to a donkey's tail was an incentive to cruelty and consequently a harmful influence on the young. His demand that the poster be withdrawn was refused.

Printed by The Dangerfield Printing Co. Ltd, London

J. Littlejohns
WHITLEY BAY
c. 1929

Printed by Haycock Press, London

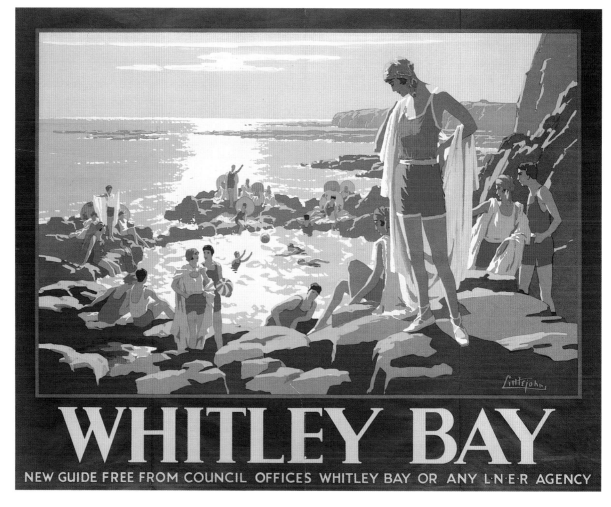

Tom Purvis
EAST COAST BY LNER
1928

This is typical of Tom Purvis' style – flat
primary colours and the elimination of
detail convey the seaside atmosphere
of the 1920s. The woman's bobbed
hair and bare arms and legs give a
youthful, carefree impression.

Printed by Sanders, Phillips & Co. Ltd, The Baynard
Press, London SW9

Laura Knight
THE YORKSHIRE COAST
1929

Printed by John Waddington Ltd, Leeds & London

THE FORTH BRIDGE

ON THE

LONDON AND NORTH EASTERN RAILWAY OF ENGLAND AND SCOTLAND

H.G. Gawthorn
THE FORTH BRIDGE
1928

The Forth Bridge crosses the estuary of the River Forth in Scotland to connect the East Coast route between London and Aberdeen. It was designed by Sir John Fowler and Sir Benjamin Baker and opened by the Prince of Wales in 1890.

Printed by David Allen & Sons Ltd, London

Andrew Johnson
FARM COLLECTION AND DELIVERY SERVICES
1928

Farmhouse collection and delivery was advertised in winter to boost goods traffic in a slack period. At this time the LNER was prepared to collect and deliver agricultural traffic within 10 miles of stations, saving the farmer time and labour. The railway companies also enjoyed a flourishing trade in farm removals.

Printed by The Dangerfield Printing Co., London

McCorquodale Studio/W.C.N.
THE GEORGE BENNIE RAILPLANE SYSTEM OF TRANSPORT
1929

The George Bennie Railplane System of Transport was a suspended monorail for passengers, set above the existing railway. Thus passenger and freight traffic was separated. The passenger cars could be either propeller-driven or electrically powered. The project, set up at Milngavie, Scotland, as an experiment, was criticized by railway traction engineers. It was funded largely by George Bennie's own considerable income, and failed because it was carelessly planned, badly conceived and took no account of technical or economic factors. George Bennie had no formal engineering education and would not take advice from those who did. The projects he devised were largely unrealistic and included proposals to build a line between Damascus and Baghdad and a route over the Sahara! He had personal assets of over £120,000 in the 1930s but was penniless by 1957 when he died. The structure for the Railplane System was dismantled in 1956.

Printed by McCorquodale, Glasgow & London

Frank Mason
THREE NEW SHIPS
1930

The LNER introduced the *SS Vienna*, *SS Amsterdam* and *SS Prague* on to its Harwich–Hook of Holland route during 1929 and 1930.

Printed by S.C. Allen & Co. Ltd, London WC2

H. G. Gawthorn
CAPACITY – MOBILITY ON THE LNER
1932

Issued in conjunction with the booklet *How the LNER "Expresses" Freight*.

Printed by The Dangerfield Printing Co. Ltd, London

Septimus E. Scott
NORTH EAST COAST EXHIBITION, NEWCASTLE-UPON-TYNE
1929

The North East Coast Exhibition was promoted by Newcastle upon Tyne as a response to the economic depression, intended both to revive trade and lift morale. It provided a showcase for the industries of the North East, attracting over four million visitors. It had its own amusement park, stadium and flower gardens, and even an African village where over a hundred Senegalese natives lived their everyday lives in mud huts for the benefit of visitors. Among the famous products that made their first appearance there were Smith's Crisps and Newcastle Exhibition Ale. The LNER had its own display and set up an information pavilion in the exhibition grounds.

Printed by Dobson Molle Ltd, Edinburgh

Austin Cooper
CRUDEN BAY
1931

The Great North of Scotland Railway opened Cruden Bay Hotel and Golf Course in 1899. Under the auspices of the LNER, Cruden Bay was widely promoted. Inclusive fare excursions were available from Aberdeen, but fewer golfers than expected were attracted. In 1932 the service to Cruden Bay was withdrawn. In 1939 the hotel was requisitioned as an army hospital. It was handed back in 1945 and sold for demolition two years later. Perhaps Cruden Bay was too far for English golfers to travel when Gleneagles and St Andrews were on the way, or perhaps the golfing season was too short and there were no other real attractions – whatever the reason, Cruden Bay was a flop.

Printed by Waterlow & Sons Ltd, London, Dunstable & Watford

Stanislaus Brien
SILLOTH ON THE SOLWAY
1932

From being almost exclusively a Scottish game for more than four hundred years, golf was adopted by the English in the nineteenth century. It had always been a traditional seaside game: the coastal turf and natural sand bunkers made for wonderful golfing country. As the game spread, there was an increasing demand by the growing middle classes for playing facilities. The railway companies saw possibilities of passengers and profit in this. Trains could transport golfers from the grime of the city to the coastal resorts, and although at first a bag of golf clubs and its owner on a railway station platform aroused curiosity, it soon became a familiar sight. The golfing girl was an invention of the Caledonian Railway and was later taken up by the LNER and LMS. Glancing through the holiday guides for the Caledonian one could be misled into thinking that golf was played predominantly by women.

Printed by Ben Johnson & Co. Ltd, York

DURHAM BY L·N·E·R

In 995 these wooded heights were chosen as the resting place of St. Cuthbert's bones—the pilgrims being guided thereto by a woman seeking a dun-cow which thereafter became a name and an emblem for the city-to-be. The church for the relics was raised in 999 and later, on the spot, the cathedral was built.

ASK FOR "THE HOLIDAY HANDBOOK" AT BOOK SELLERS AND L·N·E·R AGENCIES.   PRICE 6d

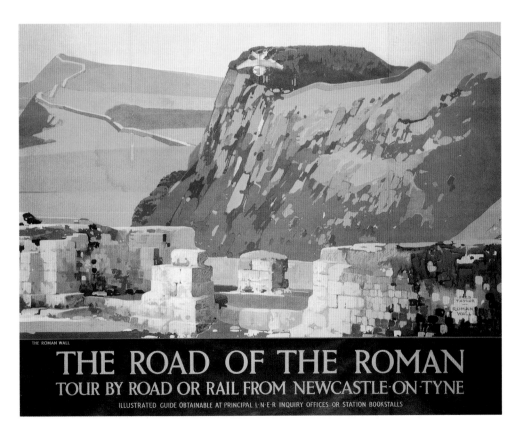

THE ROMAN WALL

THE ROAD OF THE ROMAN
TOUR BY ROAD OR RAIL FROM NEWCASTLE-ON-TYNE
ILLUSTRATED GUIDE OBTAINABLE AT PRINCIPAL L·N·E·R INQUIRY OFFICES OR STATION BOOKSTALLS

Doris Zinkeisen
DURHAM
1932

Doris and Anna Zinkeisen's railway poster work concentrated on events from history: other posters by them feature Bonnie Prince Charlie, Elizabeth I and "Scarborough in Grandmother's Day". This one shows the transfer of the relics of St Cuthbert to the site in Durham where the cathedral was later to stand. The story was fully explained in *The Holiday Handbook*.

Printed by Jarrold & Sons Ltd, Norwich & London

Fred Taylor
THE ROAD OF THE ROMAN – THE ROMAN WALL
1932

Railway posters associated with a specific historical event or place were common. This poster was issued with an accompanying guide.

Printed by The Dangerfield Printing Co. Ltd, London

Lawrence Bradshaw
KING'S CROSS FOR SCOTLAND
c. 1930

Lewis Cubitt's station at King's Cross was opened by the Great Northern Railway in 1852. It was the LNER's major departure point for the north, and many prestigious trains, including the *Flying Scotsman* and later the *Silver Jubilee* and *Coronation*, ran non-stop to the North East and Scotland.

Printed by Vincent Brooks, Day & Son Ltd, London WC2

Posters increasingly stressed the comfort of rail travel. Dining whilst travelling was not unusual, and the more prestigious trains boasted all-electric kitchens with both set and à la carte menus. The wine list on such trains as the *West Riding Limited*, the *Coronation* and the *Flying Scotsman* would not disgrace a restaurant today. In 1938 the *West Riding Limited* offered no fewer than five different kinds of champagne and nine brands of mineral water!

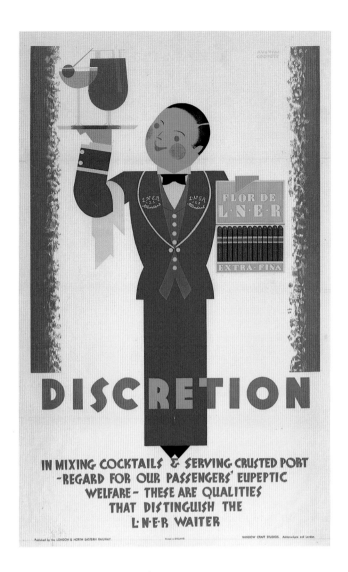

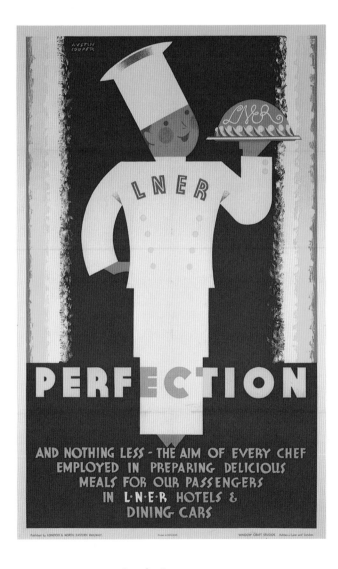

Austin Cooper
PERFECTION
1933

Austin Cooper
DISCRETION
1933

Printed by Window Craft Studios, Ashton-under-Lyne & London

Frank Newbould
ELECTRICAL PLANT ON THE LNER
1932

This modern coaling stage fed the coal from the overhead bunker to the tender (which was situated behind the locomotive and carried the fuel and water) by means of an electrically operated "jigger" or shaking conveyor. This had a slight fall towards its outlet, with a directing flap, so that the front or back of the tender could be filled without moving the engine. The aim was to speed up the handling and delivery of coal to the locomotive. The tender could be loaded in six minutes or less, depending on its capacity.

Printed by S.C. Allen & Co. Ltd, London

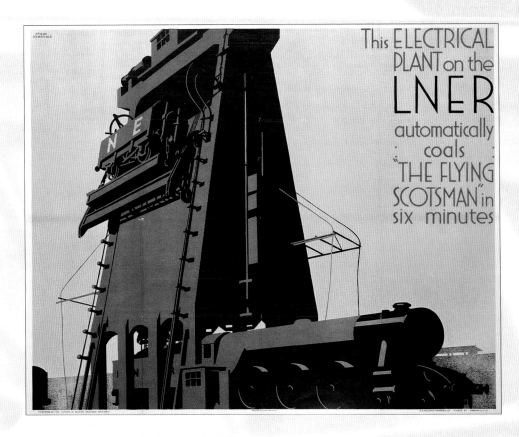

Robert Bartlett
SCOTLAND BY "THE NIGHT SCOTSMAN"
1932

Printed by S.C. Allen & Co. Ltd, London

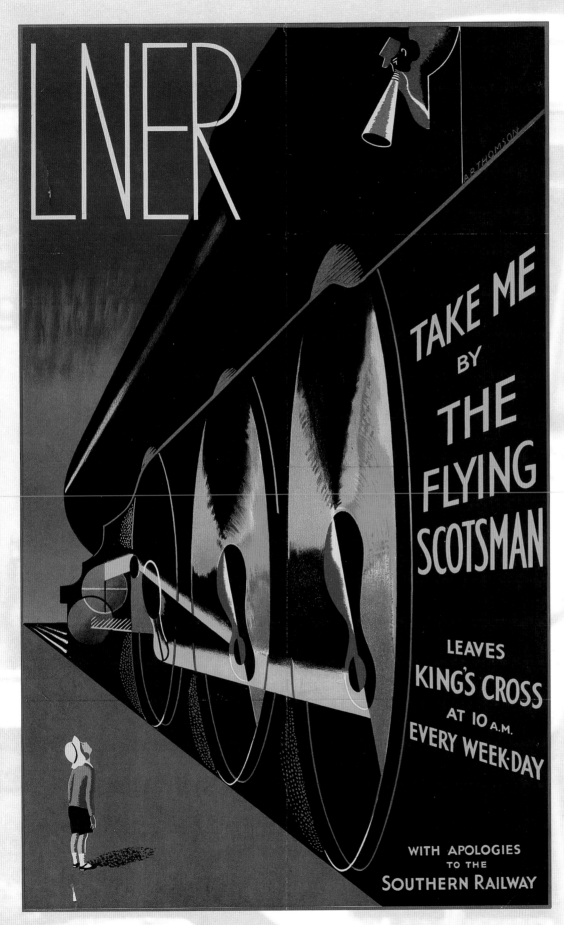

A. R. Thomson
TAKE ME BY THE FLYING SCOTSMAN
1932

A caricature of the famous Southern Railway "little boy" poster (page 77), this poked fun at the Southern's homely style. The LNER wanted to project a very different image – it considered itself to be more professional. However, for all its artistic merits, this poster was not as popular with the public as the Southern one and was not re-issued.

Printed by S.C. Allen & Co. Ltd, London

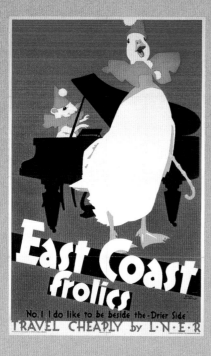

Frank Newbould
EAST COAST FROLICS
1933

No 1 'I do like to be beside the – Drier Side'
No 2 "Another perfect day" says 'the Drier Side' shellback
No 3 'Drier Side' fishing is so exciting
No 4 Col. Cottontail swears by 'The Drier Side'
No 5 'The Drier Side' scores again
No 6 'Those Drier Side Blues'

Printed by Chorley & Pickersgill Ltd, Leeds

A set of six posters exhibited in the 1933 LNER Poster Art Exhibition at the New Burlington Galleries in London. These simple posters use humour to entice the viewer to the east-coast resorts.

Frank Newbould (after John Hassall)
SKEGNESS IS SO BRACING
1933

The "Jolly Fisherman" poster "Skegness is So Bracing" is arguably the most famous English holiday poster. It was first published in 1908 by the Great Northern Railway which paid twelve pounds for it. Since then, the "Jolly Fisherman" has been caricatured over and over again and re-drawn many times. Even at its time it was an outstanding poster – most Edwardian and Victorian posters were restrained and factual. The "Skegness is So Bracing" slogan is believed to have been the idea of Mr Hiley, the Chief Passenger Agent for the Great Northern Railway. The "Jolly Fisherman" is still promoting Skegness as the ideal holiday resort; 1988 marked his eightieth birthday. John Hassall, however, died in relative obscurity in 1948.

Printed by Jarrold & Sons Ltd, Norwich & London

Dorothea Sharp
EAST COAST
1933

Printed by Chorley & Pickersgill Ltd, Leeds

Artist unknown
CAMPING COACHES
1939

The LNER sited camping coaches in its holiday districts. For a fee, a family or group could spend a week in an equipped holiday coach. The touring camping coach was a later innovation. The camping coach had the advantage of being dry, sound and free from intruding cows.

Printed by Waterlow & Sons Ltd, London & Dunstable

Gordon Nicoll
GREAT EASTERN HOTEL, LIVERPOOL ST
STATION, LONDON
1933

Printed by Haycock Press, London

Montague B. Black
EXPLORE LINCOLNSHIRE
1934

One of a series of six bird's-eye views
covering the area served by the LNER.
The other posters featured the Home
Counties, East Anglia, Yorkshire,
Northumberland and Durham and
Scotland.

Printed by McCorquodale & Co. Ltd, Glasgow &
London

LNER EDINBURGH LMS
IT'S QUICKER BY RAIL
FULL PARTICULARS FROM LNER OR LMS OFFICES AND AGENCIES

Arthur C. Michael
EDINBURGH
1936

This poster focuses on Princes Street, home of the North British Station Hotel and some of the finest shops in the city.

Printed by R.H. Perry, 20 Great Portland Street, London

W. Smithson Broadhead
SCARBOROUGH
c. 1936

The 1930s were seen by many as "Britain at its Best". This poster reflects the easy and comfortable life that was enjoyed by the better-off.

Printed by Haycock Press, London

BERWICK-UPON-TWEED
IT'S QUICKER BY RAIL
NEW GUIDE FREE FROM TOWN CLERK
OR ANY L·N·E·R AGENCY

SCARBOROUGH
IT'S QUICKER BY RAIL
FULL INFORMATION FROM L·N·E·R OFFICES AND AGENCIES

Henry Rushbury
BERWICK-UPON-TWEED
1933

Printed by Chorley & Pickersgill Ltd, Leeds

BUTLIN'S HOLIDAY CAMP
CLACTON-ON-SEA
IT'S QUICKER BY RAIL
ILLUSTRATED BOOKLET FREE FROM R. P. BUTLIN'S PUBLICITY DEPARTMENT, SKEGNESS, OR ANY L·N·E·R OFFICE OR AGENCY

EAST COAST OCCUPATIONS
BOATBUILDING
TRAIN SERVICE AND FARES TO EAST COAST RESORTS
FROM L·N·E·R STATIONS, OFFICES AND AGENCIES

J. Greenup
BUTLIN'S HOLIDAY CAMP – CLACTON-ON-SEA
1940

The inter-war years saw the rise of the holiday camp. The standard of living improved for most people, and families had more money to spend on leisure. Annual holidays became more common, and massive investment programmes were launched at popular resorts to encourage visitors. The holiday camp provided all the delights and fun of the seaside on one site. Butlin's at Clacton-on-Sea opened in June 1938 and closed at the end of the 1983 summer season.

Printed by Jarrold & Sons Ltd, Norwich & London

Frank Mason
EAST COAST OCCUPATIONS – BOATBUILDING
1947

It was appropriate that one of the last posters issued by the LNER should be by Frank Mason who had worked for them since 1923. This was one of a set of four. The others were "The Sail Loft", "The Trawl Fishers" and "The Bait Gatherers".

Printed by Jordison & Co. Ltd, London & Middlesbrough

NOTES ON ARTISTS

Compiling biographical information about commercial artists is an extremely difficult task. Unless they went on to more prestigious heights, they were largely forgotten. Many were embarrassed about having to do commercial work and used pseudonyms or did not sign their poster artwork. Several artists, including Tom Purvis, did sing the praises of industrial artistry, but they were comparatively few.

There had been little written about most poster artists, and little interest shown in their work, until the last decade. They have now gained respectability, but much vital information about them has been lost or destroyed. There is evidence available, both in the records of the four companies held at the Public Record Office and from the private papers of artists where these have survived, but it is patchy and there are still many gaps to be filled and stories told. The authors would be pleased to hear from anyone who has any information about the lifestyles, techniques and careers of the artists featured in this book.

Abbreviations

ARA Associate of the Royal Academy
ARBA Associate of the Royal Society of British Artists
ARBC Associate of the Royal British Colonial Society of Artists
ARWS Associate of the Royal Society of Painters in Water Colours
HRWS Honorary Member of the Royal Society of Painters in Water Colours
NS National Society of Painters, Sculptors and Gravers
PRBA President of the Royal Society of British Artists
PRI President of the Royal Institute of Painters in Water Colours
PRWS President of the Royal Society of Painters in Water Colours
PSWA President of the Society of Women Artists
RA Royal Academy
RBA Royal Society of British Artists
RBC Royal British Colonial Society of Artists
RDI Royal Designer for Industry
RE Royal Society of Painter-Etchers and Engravers
RI Royal Institute of Painters in Water Colours
ROI Royal Institute of Oil Painters
RP Royal Society of Portrait Painters
RSA Royal Scottish Academy

RSW Royal Scottish Society of Painters in Water Colours
RWS Royal Society of Painters in Water Colours
SGA Society of Graphic Art
SWA Society of Women Artists

BRUCE ANGRAVE (d.1983) Born in Leicester, he studied at Chiswick Art School, Ealing School of Art and the Central School of Art, London. He was a freelance book and periodical illustrator, and designed railway posters for the GWR, LMS and LNER, as well as London Transport and British Railways. **Pages 32, 120**

CHARLES H. BAKER (b.1880) Born in Ilminster and educated at Berkhamsted School, he was Head of Research at the Huntington Library, California. He painted landscapes in oil and designed posters for the LMS. **Page 114**

G. BAKER Designed posters for the GWR. **Page 49**

FRANK BALL Designed posters for the LMS. **Page 118**

WILLIAM H. BARRIBAL He worked as a figure and studio interior painter and print illustrator in London, and held regular exhibitions between 1919 and 1938. He designed railway posters for the LNER. **Page 128**

ROBERT BARTLETT Designed posters for the LNER. **Page 144**

DORA M. BATTY (c.1900–1966) She did much work for London Transport, as well as for Poole Pottery and Mac-Fisheries. From 1932 to 1958 she was a tutor in the Textiles Department at the Central School of Arts and Crafts in London. She designed posters for the GWR. **Page 43**

HENRI J. BIAIS Born in France, he designed posters for the Chemin de Fer du Nord and the SR. **Page 69**

S.J. LAMORNA BIRCH (1869–1955) Born in Cheshire, he began as an office boy and then did industrial design work for Lancashire cotton mills. He was self-taught except for a period at the Atelier Colarossi, Paris, in 1895. He took the name Lamorna from the Cornish village to distinguish himself from another painter called Birch who, like himself, was working at Newlyn. He exhibited at the Fine Art Society from 1906 and at the Royal Academy. **Page 99**

MONTAGUE BIRRELL BLACK (b.1884) Born in Stockwell, South London, he was educated at Stockwell College and concentrated on military and naval artwork. He designed posters for the LNER, LMS and SR. **Pages 101, 150**

LAWRENCE HENDERSON BRADSHAW (b.1899) He studied at Liverpool School of Art under William Penn from 1916 to 1917 and in Frank Brangwyn's studio from 1920 to 1925. As well as designing posters for the LNER, he was a sculptor. He exhibited at the Royal Academy, the Royal Society of Painters in Water Colours and other leading galleries both in London and abroad. **Page 142**

SIR FRANK WILLIAM BRANGWYN, RA, RWS (1867–1956) He studied at the South Kensington School of Art and worked in William Morris's shop in Oxford Street from 1882 to 1884. He exhibited at the Royal Academy in 1885, and from 1887 spent seven years as a sailor. Afterwards, he worked as a painter, designer and craftsman. He was a master-etcher, lithographer and painter of architectural scenes, industrial scenes and figures in oil and water-colour. He painted several murals, illustrated books and designed stained glass for St Patrick's Cathedral, Dublin. He designed posters for the LNER. **Page 126**

WILLIAM RAMSDEN BREALEY, ROI, ARBA, RSA (1889–1949) Born in Sheffield, he studied at the Sheffield School of Art and the Royal College of Art. He was a poster artist for the SR and also painted portraits. He lived in London. **Page 88**

G. STANISLAUS BRIEN A poster designer for the LNER and lino-cut artist. **Page 140**

W. SMITHSON BROADHEAD A portrait and horse painter who designed posters for the LNER and joint posters for all four companies. **Page 151**

SIR ARNESBY BROWN, RA (1866–1955) Born in Nottingham, he attended the local School of Art before going on to study under Herkomer at Bushey. He painted scenes of East Anglia and loved the countryside. He was one of the Royal Academicians employed by the LMS in 1924. He exhibited at the Venice Biennale (1934), Norwich Castle Museum (1925) and Leicester Galleries (1909). **Page 97**

F. GREGORY BROWN (1887–1948) As well as designing posters for all four railway companies, London Transport and the Empire Marketing Board, he was a landscape painter, illustrator, metal worker and textile designer. **Page 66**

P. IRWIN BROWN Designed posters for the GWR and LMS. **Page 102**

GEORGE MASSIOT BROWN Designed posters for the SR. **Page 80**

LOUIS BURLEIGH BRUHL (1861–1942) Born in Baghdad and educated in Vienna, he was principally a landscape painter and exhibited at the major London galleries from 1889. He was President of the Old Dudley Art Society and the Constable Sketching Club. Both before and after 1923 he designed railway posters for the GWR. **Pages 30, 31**

CLAUDE BUCKLE (b.1905) He was born in London and lived in Andover. Originally trained as an architect, he turned to art in 1928. He painted in both oil and watercolour and was a prolific poster artist for the GWR and British Railways. Much of his original poster artwork is held at the National Railway Museum. **Pages 38, 39, 53, 59**

JACKSON BURTON An urban landscape painter who designed posters for the LMS. **Page 109**

LESLIE CARR He painted marine subjects, architectural and river scenes, and designed posters for the SR, LNER and British Railways. **Pages 39, 80**

CASSANDRE (ADOLPHE MOURON) (1901–1968) Born in the Ukraine of French parents, he studied at the Académie Julien in Paris and adopted the pseudonym "Cassandre" after one of his lecturers. One of the few French artists who designed railway posters for the British companies, he is better known for his Dubonnet and Chemin de Fer du Nord posters. In 1930 he founded the Alliance Graphique with Charles Loupot and Maurice Moyrand. Later he produced work for American films. **Pages 69, 76**

CHRISTOPHER CLARK, RI (1875–1942) He lived in London and was a military and historical painter and illustrator. He designed posters for the LNER and LMS, and many of his designs were re-issued by British Railways. **Page 121**

ERNEST COFFIN Designed posters for the GWR and LMS. **Page 46**

AUSTIN COOPER (1890–1964) Born in Manitoba, Canada, he studied art in Cardiff before winning a scholarship to the Allan-Frazer Art College in Arbroath. He returned to Canada and began his career as a commercial artist in Montreal, but came back to London in 1922 and worked as a poster designer for the LNER, Indian State Railways and London Transport. In 1948 his first show was held at the London Gallery. **Pages 140, 143**

TERENCE TENISON CUNEO (b.1907) Son of artists Cyrus and Nell Cuneo, he studied art at the Chelsea and Slade Art Schools and has exhibited widely. As well as designing posters for the LNER, LMS and British Railways, he paints portraits (including royal portraits) and figures, ceremonial, military and railway subjects. **Page 123**

LEONARD CUSDEN Designed posters for the LNER, GWR and British Railways. **Page 51**

VERNEY L. DANVERS He ran a school of commercial art and was commissioned to work for fashion and interior design companies. He designed posters for the LNER, SR and London Transport. **Pages 71, 88, 129**

BRYAN DE GRINEAU Designed railway posters for the LMS, as well as artwork for Hornby and Meccano catalogues. **Page 117**

SIR WILLIAM RUSSELL FLINT, RA, PRWS, RSW, ROI, RE, NS (1880–1969) Born in Edinburgh, the son of a commercial artist, he studied at Daniel Stewart's College, Edinburgh, and was apprenticed as a lithographer. He studied under Hodder at the Royal Institution School of Art and was influenced by the work of Arthur Melville. He painted in Belgium, Holland and London, worked for the *Illustrated London News* from 1903 to 1907 and then illustrated Rider Haggard's *King Solomon's Mines*. In 1913 he won a silver medal at the Paris Salon and proceeded to paint throughout Europe. He was best known for his paintings of semi-nudes in France and Spain, and for landscape watercolours. **Page 35**

STANHOPE ALEXANDER FORBES, RA (1857–1947) Born in Dublin, he studied at Lambeth School of Art, the Royal Academy Schools and in Paris under Bonnat from 1874 to 1878. He painted landscapes, town scenes, coastal scenes and figures, mainly in oil. He settled in Newlyn and founded the Newlyn School of Art with his wife, Elizabeth Adela Armstrong, in 1899. He exhibited at the Royal Academy and was one of the Academicians commissioned by the LMS in 1924. **Page 96**

HENRY GEORGE GAWTHORN, SGA (1879–1941) Born in Northampton, he studied at Regent Street Polytechnic. He began his career as an architect but later turned to pictorial art. He wrote several books on poster design and publicity and produced posters for the LNER. His self-portrait can be spotted in many of his posters, complete with pince-nez and a panama hat. **Pages 130, 136, 139**

MURIEL GILL Designed posters for the GWR. **Page 51**

WARWICK GOBLE (d.1943) Born in London, he studied at Westminster School of Art. He began as a lithographer and went on to work for the *Pall Mall Gazette* and other magazines. He exhibited at the Royal Academy and other leading galleries. He illustrated many books and designed posters for the GWR and LMS. **Pages 37, 95**

J. GREENUP (d.1946) A London painter who designed posters for the LNER. **Page 152**

MAURICE WILLIAM GREIFFENHAGEN, RA, RP (1862–1931) Danish by descent, he was educated at University College School and the Royal Academy Schools. He lived in London and worked for the *Ladies Pictorial* and the *Daily Chronicle*. He also taught at the Glasgow School of Art, and exhibited in Munich, Dresden and Ghent. He decorated the British Pavilion for the Paris Exhibition in 1925. He was one of the Academicians commissioned by the LMS in 1924. **Page 13**

MURIEL HARRIS Designed posters for the SR. **Page 83**

ERNEST WILLIAM HASLEHUST, RI, RBA, RBC (1866–1949) He studied at the Slade Art School under Legros. A watercolour and landscape painter, he exhibited widely and is best remembered for his illustration of the *Beautiful Britain* series of books. He was a member of the Langham Sketching Club and the Midland Sketch Club, and designed posters for the LNER and LMS. **Page 94**

JOHN HASSALL, RI (1868–1948) The first great railway poster artist, he was born in Deal, Kent, and educated at Worthing School and Newton Abbot College. After twice failing to gain a commission at Sandhurst, he emigrated to Manitoba, Canada, but later returned to England and, after studying in Antwerp and Paris, started his own art school called the New Art School and School of Poster Design. A member of the London Sketch Club, he lived in London and designed posters for the Great Northern Railway and numerous other clients. **Page 149**

PAUL HENRY (b.1876) He was principally a landscape artist who spent most of his spare time in Ireland. He designed posters for the LMS and was their best-selling artist. **Page 104**

REGINALD EDWARD HIGGINS, ROI (1877–1933) He studied at the St John's Wood Art School and the Royal Academy Schools. He was a portrait and decorative painter who designed posters for the LNER. **Pages 107, 132**

LUDWIG HOHLWEIN (1874–1949) Born in Wiesbaden, he lived in Paris, London, Munich and Berchtesgaden. He studied as an architect and began designing posters in 1906. He also designed prospectuses, packaging and other ephemera. His early posters were for cafés, shops and restaurants in Munich; only later did he design for the LNER. He designed travel and political posters, and worked for the Nazis during the Second World War, when his style became hard and tight, reflecting Germany's cultural atmosphere in that period. **Page 133**

NORMAN HOWARD (1899–1955) He studied at the Camberwell School of Art and Westminster School of Art, and painted marine and architectural subjects. He designed posters for the LMS. **Page 98**

ERIC HESKETH HUBBARD, PRBA, ROI, RBC (1892–1957) He studied art at Heatherleys, Croydon School of Art and Chelsea Polytechnic. He painted, designed furniture and etched, and also directed the Forest Press. He was a member of the Cheltenham Group, the Society of Graver Printers, the Colour Woodcut Society and New Forest Group of Painters, and published a number of books. He designed posters for the SR. **Page 90**

ANDREW JOHNSON Designed posters for the LNER. **Page 137**

EDWARD McKNIGHT KAUFFER, HON. RDI (1890–1954) Born in Montana, USA, he studied at the Mark Hopkins Institute in San Francisco. He later studied in Paris, sponsored by Professor McKnight whose name he adopted in gratitude. He went to London in 1914 and in 1915 was commissioned by Frank Pick of the Underground Group of companies. He produced posters for the GWR and London Transport, and also designed theatre costumes, exhibition designs, interior and mural

decorations, book illustrations, carpets and textiles. He returned to America in 1940. Retrospective exhibitions of his work have been held at the Museum of Modern Art, New York and the Victoria and Albert Museum, London. **Pages 40, 43**

PATRICK COKAYNE KEELY (d.1970) Designed posters for the GWR, SR, the British and Dutch governments and London Transport. He lived in Leatherhead, Surrey. **Pages 75, 80**

T.D. KERR Designed posters for the SR. **Pages 64, 65**

DAME LAURA KNIGHT, RA, RWS, PSWA (1877–1970) She was born in Long Eaton, Derbyshire, and studied at Nottingham School of Art. From 1903 she exhibited at the Royal Academy and in 1936 became the first woman Academician. She designed posters for the LNER and London Transport, as well as designing glassware for Stuart Crystal. Her autobiography *Oil Paint and Grease Paint* was published in 1936. **Page 135**

ALFRED LAMBART (b.1902) Born in Darlington, he studied art at the Allan-Frazer Art College in Arbroath. He designed posters for the LNER and LMS, and illustrated books. **Pages 50, 103, 129**

RONALD LAMPITT Designed posters for the GWR. **Pages 44, 53**

W.E. LEADLEY Designed posters for the GWR. **Page 32**

LIBIS Designed posters for the SR. **Page 83**

LIGHT Designed posters for the LMS. **Page 120**

FREDA LINGSTROM (b.1893) After studying at the Central School of Arts and Crafts and Heatherleys, she was commissioned by the Norwegian and Swedish governments to do Scandinavian drawings for English travel propaganda. She designed posters and booklet covers for the LNER and was known for her landscape paintings. **Page 36**

JOHN LITTLEJOHNS, RI, RBA, ARBC (b.1874) Designed posters for the LNER, illustrated books for children and wrote art books. **Page 134**

SIR BERTRAM MacKENNAL, RA (1863–1931) Born in Australia, he came to England in 1933 and studied at the British Museum and at the Royal Academy Schools, and then studied in Paris. He was one of the Royal

Academicians commissioned for the LMS 1924 series. He also designed coins and was a sculptor. He returned to Australia to redecorate Government House. He was knighted in 1922 and died in Torquay. **Page 97**

WILLIAM McDOWELL Designed posters for the SR. **Page 65**

HELEN MADELEINE McKIE (d.1957) She studied at the Lambeth School of Art and lived in London, working for *The Bystander*, *The Graphic* and *The Queen* magazines. She had exhibitions at the Paris Salon and at leading galleries in London, and designed posters for the SR. **Page 91**

HELEN RAY MARSHALL Designed posters for the SR. **Page 83**

A.E. MARTIN Designed posters for the GWR. **Page 33**

FRANK HENRY MASON (1876–1965) He was educated at HMS Conway and went to sea. He painted marine and coastal subjects. As well as designing railway posters for the North Eastern Railway, GWR and LNER, he was involved in engineering and shipbuilding in Leeds and Hartlepool. He lived in Scarborough. **Pages 47, 54, 55, 130, 139, 152**

DONALD MAXWELL (1877–1936) Born in London, he studied at the Slade Art School. He worked as a naval correspondent for *The Graphic* for twenty years and was an official artist to the Admiralty during the First World War. He accompanied the Prince of Wales on his tour of India and illustrated *The Prince of Wales's Eastern Book*. He also illustrated many travel guides and books by Kipling, Hardy and Belloc, and designed posters and carriage prints for the SR. **Page 62**

CHARLES H.J. MAYO He worked in the GWR Publicity Department and produced artwork for posters, booklets and other publicity material. **Page 52**

ARTHUR C. MICHAEL A painter and etcher who worked mainly in watercolour or body colour. He illustrated books and periodicals, and designed posters for the LNER. **Page 151**

H. MOLENAAR Designed posters for the SR. **Pages 73, 74**

W.C.N. Worked for the McCorquodale Studio. **Page 137**

FRANK NEWBOULD (1887–1951) Born in Bradford, he studied at Bradford College of Art. He joined the War Office in 1942, working as an assistant to Abram Games. He designed posters for the LNER, GWR, Orient Line and Belgian Railways, and claimed to have started a landscape school in English poster design. **Pages 25, 54, 56, 57, 144, 146, 149**

GEORGE NICHOLLS Designed posters for the LMS. **Page 99**

GORDON NICOLL, RI (1888–1959) Born in London, he studied at Southampton Art School and at Hornsey under Frank Hillyard Swinstead. He was a member of the London Sketch Club. A landscape painter in watercolour and oil, he designed posters for the LNER, including a memorable series on railway hotels. **Page 150**

ALFRED JAMES OAKLEY (1878–1959) He studied at the City and Guilds School, and exhibited at the Royal Academy from 1922. As well as being a sculptor in wood and bronze, he designed posters for the LMS and LNER. **Page 109**

SIR WILLIAM NEWENHAM MONTAGUE ORPEN, RA, RWS, RI (1878–1931) Born in Ireland, he studied art at the Dublin Metropolitan School of Art and at the Slade Art School, London. He was an Official War Artist from 1917 to 1919 and was knighted in 1918. He was best known for his portrait and genre work, and was one of the Royal Academicians commissioned by the LMS in 1924. **Page 96**

CHARLES PEARS, ROI (1873–1958) Born in Pontefract and educated at East Hardwick, he became a marine painter in oil. During both the First and Second World Wars he was an Official Naval Artist. He worked as a poster artist for the LMS, LNER and the Empire Marketing Board, and was also a book illustrator. **Pages 50, 85, 86, 110, 115**

GERALD SPENCER PRYSE (1881–1956) He studied art in London and Paris, and in 1907 exhibited at the Venice International Exhibition. He lived in London and Morocco, and designed posters for the LMS and LNER. **Pages 111, 127**

J.P. Worked for the McCorquodale Studio. **Page 106**

TOM PURVIS, RDI (1888–1957) Born in Bristol, he studied at Camberwell School of Art and then went into advertising with Mather and Crowther. He worked for the LNER under William Teasdale and Charles Dandridge, as well as for Austin Reed and the British Industries Fair. He served with the Artists' Rifles in France during the First World War and became a war artist for the Ministry of Supply. In his later years he turned to religious painting. **Pages 18, 19, 131, 134, 135**

RALPH & MOTT/RALPH & BROWN Ralph & Mott was a firm of artists' agents. They employed a team of artists whose work can be found on many Great Western posters under the pseudonym Ralph Mott. Ralph & Brown were probably two of the artists from this team. Some of the artists became well known in their own right in later years. **Pages 42, 98**

LILI RÉTHI Designed posters for the LMS. **Page 117**

LEONARD RICHMOND, RBA, ROI (d.1965) He studied at the Taunton School of Art and Chelsea Polytechnic, and exhibited widely abroad as well as at the principal London galleries. He was commissioned by the Canadian government to sketch at the front in France and gather material for a large painting of Canadian soldiers constructing railways. He wrote several books on painting technique. He painted landscapes and figure subjects, and designed posters for the GWR and SR. **Pages 49, 68**

FREDERICK CAYLEY ROBINSON, ARA, RWS, ROI, RBA (1862–1922) Born in Brentford, Middlesex, he studied art at St John's Wood Art School, London, and the Académie Julien, Paris. He was one of the Royal Academicians commissioned by the LMS in 1924. He also worked as a book illustrator and mural decorator. **Page 14**

SIR HENRY GEORGE RUSHBURY (1889–1968) Born in Harborne, Birmingham, he studied art at the Birmingham College of Art and later at the Slade Art School under Henry Tonks. He was a watercolourist, etcher and drypoint artist who favoured architectural scenes. He designed posters for the LNER. **Page 151**

J.P. SAYER Designed posters for the GWR. **Page 41**

SEPTIMUS EDWIN SCOTT (b.1879) He was born in Sunderland and studied at the Royal College of Art. He designed posters for the LMS. **Pages 110, 123, 138**

MURRAY SECRETAN He worked for the LMS Advertising Department and later the Trade Advertising Section. He also worked for the Locomotive Publishing Company, painting and colouring photographs of locomotives, and designed posters for the GWR. **Page 52**

MARC FERNAND SEVERIN (b.1906) Born in Brussels, he studied art and archaeology at Ghent University. From 1932 to 1940 and 1945 to 1949 he lived in England, working first as art director of R.C. Casson advertising agency, then as a freelance artist, advertising designer and book illustrator. He designed posters for the SR. **Page 90**

EILEEN SEYD (b.1907) She studied at the Central School of Arts and Crafts. She painted in oil and watercolour, and worked as a poster artist for the SR. **Page 72**

DOROTHEA SHARP, RBA, ROI, PSWA (1874–1955) She studied art at Regent Street Polytechnic and in Paris. She lived in London and St Ives and painted landscapes and figures in oil. She designed posters for the LNER. **Page 149**

"SHEP" (CHARLES SHEPHERD) (b.1892) He studied art under Paul Woodroffe and was head of the studio at the Baynard Press. He designed posters for the Royal Mail Packet Steam Company, London Transport and the SR. Page 74.

KENNETH DENTON SHOESMITH (1890–1939) He was born in Halifax and went to sea, becoming a painter of marine subjects. He was a member of the British School of Poster Designers. **Pages 67, 68, 88**

CHARLES SIMS, RA, RWS (1873–1928) Born in London, he studied art at the Royal College of Art and in Paris, and in 1906 exhibited at the Leicester Galleries. He was an Official War Artist in 1918. He painted landscapes and figures and was an etcher, and was commissioned to work for the LMS in the 1924 Royal Academy series. He committed suicide in 1928. **Page 97**

WALTER E. SPRADBERY (1889–1969) Born in East Dulwich, London, he studied privately and joined the Society of Industrial Artists and Designers. He designed posters for the SR and London Transport. **Page 85**

FRED TAYLOR (1875–1963) Born in London, he studied at Goldsmiths' College and worked at the Waring and Gillow Studio. In 1930 he was commissioned to design four ceiling paintings for the Underwriting Room at Lloyd's and murals for Reed's Lacquer Room. He worked in naval camouflage during the Second World War. He exhibited at the Royal Academy and other galleries in London, and worked for the Empire Marketing Board, LNER, London Transport and several shipping companies. **Pages 126, 141**

A.R. THOMSON, RA, RP (b.1894) He was educated at the Royal School for the Deaf and Dumb in Margate and was an Official War Artist for the Royal Air Force during the Second World War. He was a portrait, figure and decorative artist, and painted and designed posters for the LNER. **Page 145**

G.D. TIDMARSH Designed posters for the GWR. **Page 51**

SIR HERBERT ALKER TRIPP (1883–1954) He had a long and successful career with New Scotland Yard, painting in his spare time and after his retirement. He designed posters for the GWR and SR and was knighted in 1945. **Pages 49, 84**

J.C.V. Designed posters for the SR. **Page 73**

ANTON VAN ANROOY, RI (1870–1949) Born in Holland and educated at Delft University, he studied art at the Hague Academy. He then moved to London and became a naturalized British citizen. He was a painter of portraits and interiors in oil, watercolour and pastel, and designed posters for the GWR and LNER. **Page 132**

EDMOND VAUGHAN Designed posters for the SR. **Pages 70, 73**

ARTHUR WATTS, ARBA (1883–1935) Born in Chatham, he was educated at Dulwich College and studied art at the Slade Art School and in Antwerp, Paris, Moscow and Madrid. He was a book illustrator and contracted to *Punch* and other magazines, and designed posters for the LMS. He died in a plane crash. **Page 118**

AUDREY WEBER A painter and illustrator, she was a poster artist for the SR and also illustrated SR booklets. **Pages 74, 78, 79**

F. WHATLEY A poster designer for the London and North Western Railway and LMS. **Page 101**

ETHELBERT BASIL WHITE, RWS (1891–1972) He was born in Isleworth and studied at St John's Wood Art School. He painted in watercolour and oil, illustrated books and engraved. His work was naive and figurative. He designed posters for the SR and London Transport. **Page 66**

FREDERICK JOHN WIDGERY (1861–1942) He studied at Exeter School of Art, and in Antwerp and Bushey. He painted landscapes and coastal scenes in oil and watercolour. He designed posters for the GWR. **Page 31**

NORMAN WILKINSON, PRI, ROI, HRWS (1878–1971) Born in Cambridge, he was educated at Berkhamsted School and studied art at Portsmouth and Southsea Schools of Art. A famous marine painter, he made a major contribution to the art of camouflage. He designed posters for the London and North Western Railway, LMS and SR, and organized the Royal Academy series of posters for the LMS in 1924. He also worked for the *Illustrated London News* and *Illustrated Mail*, and travelled abroad extensively. **Pages 89, 104, 106, 112, 114, 116, 122**

ANNA KATRINA ZINKEISEN, RP, ROI, NS, RDI (1901–1976) Born in Scotland, she studied at the Royal Academy Schools where she won bronze and silver medals. She designed posters for the LNER and SR. **Page 86**

DORIS CLARE ZINKEISEN, ROI (1898–1991) Like her sister, Anna Zinkeisen, she was born in Scotland and studied at the Royal Academy Schools. She lived in London and did much work for the stage, designing both sets and costumes. She designed posters for the LNER. **Page 141**

FURTHER READING

JOHN BARNICOAT, *A Concise History of Posters*, Thames and Hudson, 1972
PERCY BRADSHAW, *Art in Advertising. A Study of British and American Pictorial Publicity*, 1925
FLORENCE CAMARD and CHRISTOPHE ZAGRODZKI, *Le Train L'Affiche*, La Vie du Rail, 1989
BEVERLEY COLE and RICHARD DURACK, *Happy as a Sand-Boy*, HMSO, 1990
AUSTIN COOPER, *Making a Poster*, The Studio, 1938

OLIVER GREEN, *Underground Art*, Studio Vista, 1990
BEVIS HILLIER, *Posters*, Hamlyn Publishing Group, 1974
SYDNEY R. JONES, *Posters and their Designers*, The Studio, 1924
TOM PURVIS, *Poster Progress*, The Studio, 1939
WALTER SHAW SPARROW, *Advertising and British Art*, Bodley Head, 1924
NORMAN WILKINSON, *A Brush With Life*, Seeley, 1969

ROGER BURDETT WILSON, *Go Great Western – A History of GWR Publicity*, David and Charles, 1970

Periodicals

Commercial Art, 1922–31, which became *Commercial Art and Industry*, 1931–6, and then *Art and Industry*, 1936–47
London & North Eastern Railway Magazine, 1928–47
Railway Gazette, 1923–47
Railway Magazine, 1923–47

NATIONAL RAILWAY MUSEUM, YORK, REFERENCE NUMBERS

INTRODUCTION

Page 13
Carlisle – The Gateway to Scotland 78/38/280

Page 14
British Industries – Cotton 79/38/480

Pages 18–19
East Coast Joys
Walking Tours 78/38/46
Sun-bathing 78/38/598
Safe Sands 78/38/520
Sea Bathing 78/38/681
Sea Fishing 78/38/697
Sea Sports 78/38/699

Page 25
"The Silver Jubilee" 75/38/33

Page 30
The Shortest Route between London and Birmingham is by GWR 86/38/30
Falmouth 1990/7168

Page 31
The Cornish Riviera 87/38/281
Glorious Devon 1990/7166

Page 32
Marlborough for Downs & Forest 1990/7177
South Wales 87/38/299
Torquay 1990/7173

Page 33
Aberystwyth 81/38/51

Page 35
Chester 87/38/277
Cardiff – The City of Conferences 87/38/62
Glorious South Devon 86/38/29

Page 36
Tintern Abbey 1990/7070

Page 37
Southern Ireland 1990/7165

Page 38
Gloucester Cathedral 86/38/293
Hereford Cathedral 86/38/305

Page 39
Worcester Cathedral 86/38/53
Exeter 86/38/286

Page 40
Great Western to Devon's Moors 88/38/31

Go Great Western to Cornwall 1991/7105

Page 41
Royal Leamington Spa 88/38/53

Page 42
GWR Air Services 76/22/72

Page 43
Historic Bath 86/38/53
Royal Windsor 1991/7106
Copies of Pictorial Posters 87/38/2

Page 44
Cornwall 80/38/24
Devon 1990/7169

Page 46
London 86/38/49
Oxford 86/38/294

Page 47
London – The Tower of London 78/38/510

Page 49
Wales – Cader Idris & the Afon Mawddach 86/38/107
Southern Ireland 86/38/54
Killarney 86/38/99

Page 50
Newquay 86/38/60
The Cambrian Coast 78/38/67

Page 51
Bournemouth for Health & Pleasure 78/38/514
Clevedon – The Gem of Sunny Somerset 86/38/47
The Guide to Happy Holidays 86/38/304

Page 52
100 Years of Progress, 1835–1935 1990/7170
Speed to the West 78/38/492

Page 53
Tenby for Sunshine and Unrivalled Golden Sands 86/38/57
Plymouth, Devon 78/38/107

Page 54
London – Heart of the Empire 1989/7090
London, St Paul's 78/38/1839

Page 55
London Pride 78/38/337

Page 56
Plymouth 78/38/315

Page 57
South Devon 78/38/296
The Wye Valley 78/38/393

Page 58
Great Western Royal Hotel, Paddington, London 86/38/8

Tregenna Castle Hotel, St Ives, Cornwall 86/38/302

Page 59
Weston Super-Mare 83/38/85

Page 62
Dorset Coast 87/38/285
The "Lake District" of Surrey 86/38/28

Page 64
Progress Posters No 1 – Electrification! 86/38/15
No 2 – Steam! 86/38/14

Page 65
No 3 – The Viaduct 86/38/13
Cross the Atlantic by White Star 87/38/295

Page 66
The Londoner's Garden, Kent 88/38/34
Kentish Hills & Surrey Dales 88/38/94

Page 67
Eastbourne 1989/7141

Page 68
Glorious Holidays Abroad – Venice 1991/7443
The "Golden Arrow" Service and the "Motorist's" Service leaving Dover 87/38/69

Page 69
Nord Express 1991/7102
Vers L'Angleterre via Calais–Douvres ou Boulogne–Folkestone 1990/7157

Page 70
South for Winter Sunshine 86/38/6

Page 71
Ensure a Good Morning 88/38/136
Enjoy a Good Night 88/38/137

Page 72
You May be Moving! 78/38/970
For your Shopping – Cheap Day Tickets 78/38/967

Page 73
South for Sunshine 1990/7063
Winter Sunshine 83/38/320
So Swiftly Home 1991/7445

Page 74
Bournemouth Belle 88/38/138
Brighton Belle 86/38/36
Winter Sports Expresses 87/38/288

Page 75
Southern for the Continent 85/38/25

Page 76
New Night Service 88/38/125

Page 77
I'm Taking An Early Holiday 'Cos I Know Summer Comes Soonest in the South 75/38/41
Si, Sono Venuto in Inghilterra 78/38/974

Page 78
Conducted Rambles – Spring 78/38/993

Page 79
Conducted Rambles – Summer 78/38/996
Conducted Rambles – Autumn 78/38/933

Page 80
Southampton Central Station 78/38/989
While *you* sleep, London–Paris by Train–Ferry 79/38/320
Southampton Docks 78/38/97

Page 83
To Your Libraries, Lectures, Museums 1990/7064
"Hints for Holidays" (little boy) 78/38/936
(waterskier) 78/38/977

Page 84
Fresh Air for Health! 78/38/468

Page 85
Summer Services for Winter Visitors to Portsmouth, Southsea & Isle of Wight 75/38/37
The South Downs 78/38/150

Page 86
The White Cliffs of Dover 86/38/58
"Sunset over Guernsey" 76/38/20

Page 88
Ramsgate 87/38/109
Why Do They Call Me Sunny South Sam? 78/38/39
Folkestone 78/38/976

Page 89
The New TS "Falaise" 78/38/57

Page 90
The Devon Belle 78/38/106
See the West Country from the Train 78/38/398

Page 91
Waterloo Station – War 76/38/66
Waterloo Station – Peace
76/38/67

Page 94
Sweet Rothesay Bay 1991/7097
Alton Towers and Gardens
82/38/41

Page 95
Stratford-upon-Avon 78/38/79

Page 96
The Night Mail – The
Enginemen 78/38/8
The Permanent Way – Relaying
76/38/37

Page 97
Nottingham Castle – The Centre
of Mediaeval England
86/38/253
London 79/38/455
Speed 78/38/227

Page 98
Find Radiant Health at
Llandrindod-Wells 86/38/307
Scotland – Straight as The Crow
Flies 86/38/11

Page 99
The Highlands in Winter
88/38/10
Buxton 88/38/97

Page 101
Spend Your Holidays in the Lake
District 86/38/310
Ingleton – The Land of
Waterfalls 88/38/39

Page 102
A Total Eclipse of the Sun
88/38/78
Liverpool & Manchester Railway
Centenary Celebrations
1989/70

Page 103
Spend a day at Port Sunlight
87/38/67

Page 104
Golf in Northern Ireland – The
8th Green at Portrush 78/38/58
Connemara 1989/7139

Page 105
Perry Barr, Birmingham – "The
Goodwood of Greyhound
Racing" 1991/7088

Page 106
Regular Services between Goole

and Hamburg, Amsterdam,
Rotterdam, Antwerp, Ghent,
Dunkerque, Copenhagen
87/38/66
Put Your Plant Where It Will
Grow 88/38/54

Page 107
Isle of Man – The Landing of
King Orry 1989/7116

Page 108
Spend Your Summer Holidays at
Blackpool in June 1991/7132

Page 109
Vale of the Usk 88/38/25
Sunny Rhyl – The Children's
Paradise 86/38/38

Page 110
Lytham St. Annes 1990/7088
New Brighton & Wallasey
79/38/472

Page 111
The Famous Bathing Pool at
Hastings & St Leonards
88/38/105

Page 112
"Royal Scot" leaves Euston
86/38/279

Page 113
Midland Hotel, Morecambe
86/38/280
North Stafford Hotel, Stoke-on-
Trent 86/38/276

Page 114
Britannia Tubular Bridge, Menai
Straits 78/38/331
Snowdonia 82/38/40

Page 115
Southend-on-Sea – Night Scene
off Pierhead 78/38/64

Page 116
Tilbury for the Continent
78/38/326
Launch of TSS Duke of York.
Queen's Island, Belfast
88/38/57

Page 117
The Coronation Scot 81/38/6
Crewe Works – Building
"Coronation" Class Engines
85/38/59

Page 118
Grange Over Sands 1989/7123
A Map of the Lake District
78/38/450

Page 120
Come to Cromer 1991/7086
Crystal Palace Road Circuit –
Grand Composite Meeting
1990/7033

Page 121
London – St. James's Palace
83/38/97

Page 122
Harrow School 78/38/345
Repton School 85/38/61

Page 123
The Day Begins 76/38/30
Your Friends on the LMS
85/38/57

Page 126
Over the Nidd near Harrogate
88/38/58
York Minster – England's
Treasure House of Stained
Glass 1990/7061
London 86/38/352

Page 127
The Broads 87/38/80

Page 128
Bridlington 78/38/178

Page 129
Try a Fly 87/38/144
Tynemouth 88/38/89

Page 130
Great Yarmouth & Gorleston on
Sea 78/38/475
Remember East Anglia Next
Summer 1991/7121

Page 131
The Trossachs – Ellen's Isle, Loch
Katrine 86/38/333

Page 132
Belgium, Harwich–Zeebrugge
87/38/52
Olympic Games, Amsterdam
87/38/134

Page 133
Munich and Central Europe
78/38/220

Page 134
Mablethorpe & Sutton-on-Sea
1990/7267
Whitley Bay 78/38/223

Page 135
The Yorkshire Coast 86/38/414
East Coast by LNER 86/38/340

Page 136
The Forth Bridge 1989/7142

Page 137
Farm Collection and Delivery
Services 86/38/395
The George Bennie Railplane
System of Transport 76/38/21

Page 138
North East Coast Exhibition,

Newcastle-upon-Tyne 1991/
7144

Page 139
Three New Ships 75/38/23
Capacity – Mobility on the LNER
84/38/54

Page 140
Silloth on the Solway 1990/7068
Cruden Bay 86/38/394

Page 141
Durham 86/38/430
The Road of the Roman – The
Roman Wall 86/38/350

Page 142
King's Cross for Scotland
88/38/88

Page 143
Perfection 1991/7103
Discretion 88/38/91

Page 144
Electrical Plant on the LNER
86/38/374
Scotland by "The Night
Scotsman" 88/38/115

Page 145
Take Me by The Flying Scotsman
77/38/11

Page 146
East Coast Frolics
No 1 'I do like to be beside the –
Drier Side' 78/38/627
No 2 "Another perfect day" says
'the Drier Side' shellback
78/38/688
No 3 'Drier Side' fishing is so
exciting 78/38/682
No 4 Col. Cottontail swears by
'The Drier Side' 78/38/687
No 5 'The Drier Side' scores
again 78/38/714
No 6 'Those Drier Side Blues'
78/38/715

Page 149
East Coast 86/38/423
Skegness is So Bracing 88/38/99
Camping Coaches 78/38/44

Page 150
Great Eastern Hotel, Liverpool St
Station, London 86/38/429
Explore Lincolnshire 78/38/208

Page 151
Edinburgh 86/38/454
Berwick-upon-Tweed 1990/7081
Scarborough 78/38/222

Page 152
Butlin's Holiday Camp – Clacton-
on-Sea 86/38/404
East Coast Occupations –
Boatbuilding 78/38/669